FIX IT QUICK™
gifts from your
KITCHEN

Publications International, Ltd.

Favorite Brand Name Recipes at www.fbnr.com

Front cover photography by Proffitt Photography Ltd., Chicago.

Pictured on the front cover *(clockwise from top):* Cherries and Cream Muffins *(page 164)*, Happy Birthday Cookies *(page 22)*, Reese's® Peanut Butter and Milk Chocolate Chip Brownies *(page 152)*, White Truffles *(page 44)* and Lemon Cranberry Loaf *(page 174)*.

Pictured on the back cover *(left to right):* Colorful Cookie Buttons *(page 122)*, White Truffles *(page 44)* and Tex-Mex Quick Bread *(page 169)*.

ISBN: 1-4127-2236-5

Library of Congress Control Number: 2005924028

Manufactured in China.

8 7 6 5 4 3 2 1

Microwave Cooking: Microwave ovens vary in wattage. Use the cooking times as guidelines and check for doneness before adding more time.

Preparation/Cooking Times: Preparation times are based on the approximate amount of time required to assemble the recipe before cooking, baking, chilling or serving. These times include preparation steps such as measuring, chopping and mixing. The fact that some preparations and cooking can be done simultaneously is taken into account. Preparation of optional ingredients and serving suggestions is not included.

Contents

Top to bottom: Donna's Heavenly Orange Chip Scones (page 170), Banana Snack Cake (page 20) and Praline Pecans & Cranberries (page 70)

Get Back to Basics

No matter what you're preparing, beautiful food starts with good cooking and baking basics. Here are some guidelines to keep in mind.

• Before beginning, read the entire recipe to make sure you have all the necessary ingredients, utensils and supplies.

• For best results, use the ingredients called for in the recipe. For example, butter, margarine and shortening are not always interchangeable.

• Measure ingredients accurately and assemble them in the order they are called for in the recipe.

• Follow the recipe directions and cooking or baking times exactly. Check for doneness using the test given in the recipe.

• Always use the pan or dish size specified in the recipe. Using a different size may cause under or overcooking, or sticking and burnt edges.

• Before baking, adjust the oven racks and preheat the oven. Check the oven temperature for accuracy with an oven thermometer.

Cocoa Raisin-Chip Cookies (page 36)

The Perfect Package

Homemade goodies from your kitchen are a thoughtful gift for any occasion. Make your food gifts extraordinary by wrapping them in unique packages and using decorative accessories. Remember to always use food-safe containers with airtight lids and make sure containers are completely dry before filling them with food or ingredients.

Airtight Canisters: These containers are available in a variety of materials, including glass and plastic. They are great for storing snack mixes, cookies and candies.

Baskets & Boxes: These versatile hold-alls are available in a wide variety of materials and sizes. Wrap plain boxes in decorative papers. Large, sturdy baskets and boxes are well-suited for packing entire themed gifts.

Glass Bottles: Airtight bottles are perfect for barbecue or other types of sauces. Always choose securely stoppered bottles to help prevent leakage.

Glass Jars: Jars are wonderful for presenting jams, snack mixes, and soup and cookie mixes. Make sure that the jars have airtight lids.

Gift Bags: These handy totes come in a wide variety of sizes, colors and shapes. Pack individual cookies and candies in smaller bags; pack goody-filled jars, canisters or bottles in larger bags.

Tins: Metal containers with tight-fitting lids are just the right choice for snack mixes, cookies, truffles and other candies. They also hold up well when sent through the mail.

Finishing Touches

After the goodies are made and packaged, you're ready to put the finishing touches on your gift.

Cellophane: This is an indispensable material for hard-to-wrap gifts such as individual breads and candies. Gather the ends and secure with a multitude of pretty ribbons.

Decorative Papers: Papers come in a variety of finishes and many can be enhanced with rubber stamps. Colorful tissue papers are perfect for tucking into gift boxes and bags.

Gift Tags: Tags come in handy when making personalized notes or cards. They also make great labels for storing directions or the recipe itself.

Raffia: Tuck assorted colors of raffia into boxes, baskets and pails. Or, use it as ribbon and tie boxes and tins with rustic bows.

Ribbons, Satin Cords and Strings: Thick, colorful ribbons, metallic strings and thin shiny cords add a touch of glamour to any kind of wrapping paper.

Rubber Stamps: Stamps with food or holiday themes paired with colorful inks are perfect for decorating plain papers. They are also great for making personalized note cards for recipes, labels for jams, storing directions and gift tags.

Special Instructions

Before giving your gifts, remember to include storage directions for perishable items, especially those that must be refrigerated. It is also nice to include serving suggestions with food gifts, or even the recipe itself.

Special Delivery

When sending edible gifts, proper food selection and packaging is very important.

• Moist quick breads and sturdy cookies are ideal choices, as are many non-fragile confections such as fudge and caramels.

• Brownies and bar cookies are generally sturdy but avoid shipping those with moist fillings and frostings since they become sticky at room temperature. For the same reason, shipping anything with chocolate during the summer or to warm climates is risky.

• When sending cookies, wrap each type of cookie separately to retain flavors and textures. Cookies can also be wrapped back-to-back in pairs with either plastic wrap or foil.

• It is best to prepare foods just before packing and mailing. Foods should be completely cool before wrapping and packing.

• Always wrap all breakable containers in bubble wrap.

• Fill the bottom of a sturdy shipping box with an even layer of packing material. Do not use popped popcorn or puffed cereal as it may attract insects. Place the wrapped foods or containers as snugly as possible inside. Then place crumpled waxed paper, newspaper or paper toweling in between the individual wrapped foods or containers. Fill any crevices with packing material, and add a final layer at the top of the box.

• Ship your food gifts to arrive as soon as possible.

Gourmet Gifts in a Jar

Present loved ones with a pretty layered jar filled with the ingredients to make soup, muffins, cookies or snacks. Or surprise them with a homemade jam, pesto or hot fudge sauce. It's the perfect gift to show just how much you care.

Mystical Bars Mix

> **1 cup graham cracker crumbs**
> **1 cup coarsely chopped pecans**
> **¾ cup flaked coconut**
> **¾ cup semisweet chocolate chips**
> **½ cup uncooked old-fashioned or quick oats**
> **½ cup raisins**

1. Layer ingredients attractively in any order in 1-quart food storage jar with tight-fitting lid. Pack ingredients down tightly before adding another layer.

2. Seal jar. Cover top of jar with 8-inch circle of fabric, if desired; attach recipe gift tag with raffia or ribbon. *Makes one 1-quart jar*

Mystical Bars

> **⅓ cup butter**
> **1 jar Mystical Bars Mix**
> **1 can (14 ounces) sweetened condensed milk**

1. Preheat oven to 350°F. Melt butter in 13×9-inch baking pan. Remove from oven.

2. Place contents of jar in large bowl. Add sweetened condensed milk; stir with spoon until well blended.

3. Spread batter evenly in prepared pan. Bake 22 to 25 minutes or until lightly browned. Cool in pan on wire rack 5 minutes. Cut into bars. Cool completely in pan on wire rack. *Makes 2½ dozen bars*

Mystical Bars

Spicy Chili Mac Mix

¾ **cup dried pinto beans**
¾ **cup dried red kidney beans**
1 **package (about 1¼ ounces) chili**
     seasoning mix
2 **tablespoons dried minced onion**
2 **teaspoons beef bouillon granules**
¼ **teaspoon red pepper flakes**
1½ **cups uncooked rotini pasta**

1. Layer pinto and kidney beans in 1-quart food storage jar with tight-fitting lid. Combine chili seasoning mix, onion, bouillon granules and pepper flakes in small plastic food storage bag; close bag with twist tie. Place on top of beans spreading out bag to cover beans. Place pasta on top of bag.

2. Seal jar. Cover top of jar with 8-inch circle of fabric, if desired; attach recipe gift tag with raffia or ribbon. *Makes one 1-quart jar*

Helpful Hint

An easy way to fill gift jars with mixes is to use a canning funnel and a ¼-cup dry measuring cup. Also, for make-ahead gifts that can be stored until needed, fill several jars at one time.

Spicy Chili Mac

1 **jar Spicy Chili Mac Mix**
4 **to 5 cups water**
2 **cans (14½ ounces each) diced tomatoes**
     with green chilies, undrained
1 **pound ground beef or ground turkey,**
     browned and drained
     Shredded Cheddar cheese (optional)

1. Remove pasta and seasoning packet from jar; set aside.

2. Place beans in large bowl; cover with water. Soak 6 to 8 hours or overnight. (To quick soak beans, place beans in large saucepan; cover with water. Bring to a boil over high heat. Boil 2 minutes. Remove from heat; let soak, covered, 1 hour.) Drain beans; discard water.

3. Combine soaked beans, water, tomatoes with juice, ground beef and contents of seasoning packet in Dutch oven. Bring to a boil over high heat. Cover; reduce heat and simmer 1½ hours. Add pasta and simmer 30 to 45 minutes. Sprinkle with Cheddar cheese, if desired. *Makes 8 to 10 servings*

Spicy Chili Mac

Nutty Orzo and Rice Pilaf Mix

**¾ cup uncooked orzo pasta
3 tablespoons dried vegetable flakes, soup greens or dehydrated vegetables
2 teaspoons chicken bouillon granules
½ teaspoon dried thyme leaves
¼ teaspoon black pepper
½ cup uncooked instant brown rice
½ cup pecans pieces**

1. Layer orzo, vegetable flakes, bouillon granules, thyme, pepper and rice in 1-pint food storage jar with tight-fitting lid. Place pecans in small plastic food storage bag; close with twist tie. Cut off top of bag. Place bag on top of rice.

2. Seal jar. Cover top of jar with 6-inch circle of fabric, if desired; attach recipe gift tag with raffia or ribbon. *Makes one 1-pint jar*

Note: Vegetable Flakes and Soup Greens made by McCORMICK® are available in the spice section of large supermarkets. If these products are not available, ask your grocer to order them. Also, look for dried vegetable flakes (bell peppers, carrots, etc.) in the bulk food section of specialty food markets such as natural or bulk food stores.

Nutty Orzo and Rice Pilaf

**1 jar Nutty Orzo and Rice Pilaf Mix
2 cups water
1 tablespoon butter**

1. Preheat oven to 350°F. Remove pecan packet from jar; set aside.

2. Combine water, butter and remaining contents of jar in large saucepan. Bring to a boil over high heat. Cover; reduce heat and simmer 10 to 15 minutes or until orzo is tender.

3. Meanwhile, spread pecans in single layer on ungreased cookie sheet; bake 5 to 8 minutes or until nuts just begin to darken.

4. Stir pecans into pilaf. Cook, uncovered, 2 to 3 minutes or until heated through.
Makes 4 to 5 servings

Variations: Add 1 cup cooked peas and carrots *or* ½ cup drained canned sliced mushrooms in step 4. Heat through.

Nutty Orzo and Rice Pilaf

Luscious Orange Cranberry Scone Mix

1 cup all-purpose flour
¾ cup dried cranberries or dried
** blueberries**
½ cup packed brown sugar
¼ cup granulated sugar
1 cup all-purpose flour
2 teaspoons baking powder
½ teaspoon ground ginger
½ teaspoon ground cinnamon
¼ teaspoon baking soda
¼ teaspoon salt
½ cup powdered sugar

1. Layer all ingredients except powdered sugar in order listed above in 1-quart food storage jar with tight-fitting lid. Pack ingredients down lightly before adding another layer. Place powdered sugar in small plastic food storage bag; close with twist tie. Cut off top of bag. Place bag in jar.

2. Seal jar. Cover top of jar with 8-inch circle of fabric, if desired; attach recipe gift tag with raffia or ribbon. *Makes one 1-quart jar*

Gift Idea: Assemble a napkin-lined gift basket with a jar of Luscious Orange Cranberry Scone Mix, oranges and a package of premium coffee or tea. Add a nonstick silicone baking mat for the gourmet cook.

Luscious Orange Cranberry Scones

1 jar Luscious Orange Cranberry Scone Mix
6 tablespoons (¾ stick) butter, cut into pieces
** and softened**
½ cup buttermilk
1 egg
2 teaspoons grated orange or lemon peel
1 teaspoon orange or lemon extract
2 to 3 teaspoons orange or lemon juice

1. Preheat oven to 350°F. Lightly grease baking sheet.

2. Remove powdered sugar packet from jar. Place remaining contents of jar in large bowl. Cut in butter with pastry blender or 2 knives until mixture resembles coarse crumbs. Whisk together buttermilk, egg, orange peel and orange extract in small bowl. Add buttermilk mixture to flour mixture; stir until stiff dough is formed. Knead dough in bowl. Drop by ¼ cupfuls onto prepared baking sheet.

3. Bake 18 to 20 minutes or until toothpicks inserted into centers come out clean. Remove to wire racks; cool 10 minutes.

4. Stir together powdered sugar and enough orange juice to make glaze. Drizzle over scones. Serve warm.
Makes 12 scones

Luscious Orange Cranberry Scones

Green & Yellow Split Pea Soup Mix

¾ cup dried green split peas
¾ cup dried yellow split peas
1 bay leaf
1 package dry vegetable soup and dip mix
1 teaspoon chicken bouillon granules
½ teaspoon lemon pepper

1. Layer green and yellow split peas in 1-pint food storage jar with tight-fitting lid. Slide bay leaf down side of jar. Combine soup and dip mix, bouillon granules and lemon pepper in small plastic food storage bag; close with twist tie. Cut off top of bag. Place bag on top of peas.

2. Seal jar. Cover top of jar with 6-inch circle of fabric, if desired; attach recipe gift tag with raffia or ribbon. *Makes one 1-pint jar*

Gift Idea: Assemble a jar of Green & Yellow Split Pea Soup Mix with a package of corn bread mix in a decorative gift basket or bag.

Green & Yellow Split Pea Soup

1 jar Green & Yellow Split Pea Soup Mix
5 to 6 cups water
1 to 2 smoked ham hocks *or* 1 meaty ham bone

1. Remove seasoning packet and bay leaf from jar; set aside.

2. Sort and rinse peas thoroughly. Combine peas, water, ham hock, contents of seasoning packet and bay leaf in slow cooker. Cover and cook on LOW 4 to 5 hours or until peas are tender.

3. Remove and discard bay leaf. Take out ham hock; remove skin and cut meat from bones in chunks. Return meat to slow cooker. Heat through.
Makes 4 to 5 servings

Conventional Method: In step 2, simmer bean mixture in Dutch oven, partially covered, 1 hour or until tender. Continue as directed in step 3.

Green & Yellow Split Pea Soup

Festive Cranberry Waffle Mix

- ¾ **cup all-purpose flour**
- 2 **teaspoons baking powder**
- 1 **teaspoon dried orange peel**
- ½ **teaspoon baking soda**
- ½ **teaspoon ground cinnamon**
- ¼ **teaspoon salt**
- ⅓ **cup yellow cornmeal**
- ⅓ **cup sugar**
- ½ **cup dried cranberries or dried cherries, coarsely chopped**
- ¼ **cup all-purpose flour**

1. Layer all ingredients in order listed above in 1-pint food storage jar with tight-fitting lid. Pack ingredients down tightly before adding another layer.

2. Seal jar. Cover top of jar with 6-inch circle of fabric, if desired; attach recipe gift tag with raffia or ribbon. *Makes one 1-pint jar*

Gift Idea: Assemble a brunch gift basket with jar of Festive Cranberry Waffle Mix, a bottle of maple syrup, a package of gourmet ground coffee and 8 juice oranges. For a more elaborate gift, include a waffle iron.

Festive Cranberry Waffles

- 1 **jar Festive Cranberry Waffle Mix**
- 1 **cup buttermilk**
- ¼ **to ½ cup milk or orange juice, divided**
- 1 **egg**
- 1 **teaspoon vanilla**
- 3 **tablespoons butter, melted**
  Toppings: Butter, maple syrup and powdered sugar (optional)

1. Preheat waffle iron.

2. Place contents of jar in large bowl; stir until well blended. Whisk together buttermilk, ¼ cup milk, egg and vanilla in medium bowl. Add to jar mixture; stir until just moistened. Stir in melted butter. Add additional milk, 1 tablespoon at a time, if batter is too thick.

3. Spray waffle iron with nonstick cooking spray. Spoon about ¾ cup batter* onto iron. Close lid; bake until steaming stops or waffles are brown and crispy. Serve immediately with desired toppings.
Makes 4 (7-inch) round waffles

*Check manufacturer's directions for recommended amount of batter and baking time.

Festive Cranberry Waffle

No-Cook Strawberry Jam

2 quarts ripe strawberries, hulled
¼ cup lemon juice
1 package (2 ounces) powdered fruit
     pectin
1 cup KARO® Light Corn Syrup
4½ cups sugar

1. In blender or food processor finely chop strawberries. Measure 3¼ cups.

2. In 4-quart bowl combine measured fruit and lemon juice. Slowly add pectin, stirring vigorously. Let stand 30 minutes, stirring occasionally.

3. Add corn syrup; stir until well combined. Gradually stir in sugar until dissolved.

4. Ladle into ½-pint freezer jars or containers, leaving ½-inch headspace; cover tightly. Refrigerate jams to be used in 2 to 3 weeks; freeze up to 1 year.   *Makes about 4 pints*

Peach or Nectarine Jam: Omit strawberries. Peel and pit about 2½ pounds ripe peaches or nectarines. Finely chop in blender or food processor. Measure 3¼ cups; complete as directed in steps 2, 3 and 4.

Apricot Jam: Omit strawberries. Peel and pit about 3 pounds ripe apricots. Finely chop in blender or food processor. Measure 3¼ cups; complete as directed in steps 2, 3 and 4.

Apricot Raspberry Jam: Omit strawberries. Peel and pit about 1½ pounds ripe apricots. Finely chop in blender or food processor. Measure 2 cups. Fully crush 1 to 2 pints ripe raspberries. Measure 1½ cups. Combine with measured apricots; complete as directed in steps 2, 3 and 4.

Sweet Cherry Jam: Omit strawberries. Pit about 2½ pounds ripe sweet cherries. Finely chop in blender or food processor. Measure 3¼ cups; complete as directed in steps 2, 3 and 4.

Gooey Hot Fudge Sauce

2 cups (12 ounces) semisweet chocolate
     chips
2 tablespoons butter
½ cup half-and-half
1 tablespoon corn syrup
⅛ teaspoon salt
½ teaspoon vanilla

Combine chocolate, butter, half-and-half, corn syrup and salt in heavy 2-quart saucepan over low heat. Cook and stir until chocolate is melted and mixture is smooth. Remove from heat; let cool 10 minutes. Stir in vanilla. Serve warm or pour into clean glass food storage jars and seal tightly. Store up to 6 months in refrigerator. Reheat sauce in double-boiler over hot (not boiling) water before serving, if desired.
   Makes about 1½ cups sauce

Parmesan Ranch Party Mix

2 cups bite-size corn or rice cereal
2 cups (½ package) bagel chips, broken in half
1½ cups pretzel twists
1 cup oyster crackers
1 cup pistachio nuts
¼ cup grated Parmesan cheese
1 package (1 ounce) dry ranch salad dressing mix
½ teaspoon garlic powder
⅛ teaspoon ground red pepper

1. Layer cereal, bagel chips, pretzels, crackers, nuts and cheese attractively in any order in 2-quart food storage jar with tight-fitting lid. Combine dressing mix, garlic powder and red pepper in small plastic food storage bag; close with twist tie. Cut off top of bag. Place bag in jar.

2. Seal jar. Cover top of jar with 8-inch circle of fabric, if desired; attach recipe gift tag with raffia or ribbon.   *Makes one 2-quart jar*

Gift Idea: Assemble a gift basket with a jar of Parmesan Ranch Party Mix and a favorite beverage (beer, wine or soda).

Parmesan Ranch Party Mix

1 jar Parmesan Ranch Party Mix
¼ cup (½ stick) butter

1. Preheat oven to 300°F. Remove seasoning packet from jar. Place remaining contents of jar in large bowl. Melt butter in small saucepan. Add contents of seasoning packet; stir until blended. Drizzle over cereal mixture; toss to coat.

2. Spread mixture in single layer on ungreased jelly-roll pan. Bake 20 to 30 minutes or until mixture is lightly browned, stirring every 10 minutes. Cool completely in pan on wire rack. Store in airtight container at room temperature up to 2 weeks.
Makes about 6 cups party mix

Variation: Stir 1 cup dried cranberries into cooled mix for a colorful variation.

Banana Snack Cake Mix

1¼ cups all-purpose flour
1 cup semisweet chocolate chips
¾ cup packed light brown sugar
½ cup granulated sugar
½ cup chopped walnuts
1 teaspoon baking powder
¾ teaspoon salt
½ teaspoon baking soda

1. Layer ingredients in any order in 1-quart food storage jar with tight-fitting lid. Pack ingredients down lightly before adding another layer.

2. Seal jar. Cover top of jar with 8-inch circle of fabric, if desired; attach recipe gift tag with raffia or ribbon.   *Makes one 1-quart jar*

Banana Snack Cake

1 jar Banana Snack Cake Mix
1¼ cups mashed ripe bananas (about 4 medium)
½ cup vegetable oil
2 eggs, beaten
1 teaspoon vanilla

1. Preheat oven to 350°F. Grease and flour 8- or 9-inch square baking pan.

2. Place jar contents in large bowl. Stir in bananas, oil, eggs and vanilla until blended. Pour into prepared pan.

3. Bake 40 to 45 minutes or until toothpick inserted into center comes out clean. Cool completely in pan on wire rack.   *Makes 9 to 12 servings*

Cranberry Pecan Muffin Mix

1¾ cups all-purpose flour
1 cup dried cranberries
¾ cup chopped pecans
½ cup packed light brown sugar
2½ teaspoons baking powder
½ teaspoon salt

1. Layer ingredients in any order in 1-quart food storage jar with tight-fitting lid. Pack ingredients down lightly before adding another layer.

2. Seal jar. Cover top of jar with 8-inch circle of fabric, if desired; attach recipe gift tag with raffia or ribbon.   *Makes one 1-quart jar*

Cranberry Pecan Muffins

1 jar Cranberry Pecan Muffin Mix
¾ cup milk
¼ cup (½ stick) butter, melted
1 egg, beaten

1. Preheat oven to 400°F. Grease or paper-line 12 standard (2½-inch) muffin pan cups.

2. Place contents of jar in large bowl. Combine milk, melted butter and egg in small bowl until blended; stir into jar mixture just until moistened. Spoon evenly into prepared muffin cups.

3. Bake 16 to 18 minutes or until toothpicks inserted into centers come out clean. Cool in pan on wire rack 5 minutes. Remove from pan; cool completely on wire rack.   *Makes 12 muffins*

Banana Snack Cake

1 jar Banana Snack Cake Mix
1¼ cups mashed ripe bananas
   (about 4 medium)
½ cup vegetable oil

2 eggs, beaten
1 teaspoon vanilla
Chocolate frosti...

1. Preheat oven to 350°F. Grease and flour 9×9-inch bakin...
2. Place contents of jar in large bowl. Add bananas, oil
   until well blended. Pour in ...pared pan.
3. Bake 40 to 45 minutes until ...ick in...

Cool completely in p...

Mak... 9 to 12 servings

Banana Snack Cake

Happy Birthday Cookie Mix

1¼ cups flour
½ teaspoon baking powder
¼ teaspoon baking soda
¼ teaspoon salt
⅓ cup packed brown sugar
⅓ cup granulated sugar
½ cup chocolate-covered toffee chips
¾ cup mini candy-coated chocolate pieces
½ cup peanut butter and milk chocolate chips
½ cup lightly salted peanuts, coarsely chopped

1. Combine flour, baking powder, baking soda and salt in large bowl. Spoon flour mixture into 1-quart food storage jar with tight-fitting lid. Layer remaining ingredients on top of flour. Pack ingredients down lightly before adding another layer.

2. Seal jar. Cover top of jar with 8-inch circle of fabric, if desired; attach recipe gift tag with raffia or ribbon. *Makes one 1-quart jar*

Happy Birthday Cookies

½ cup (1 stick) butter, softened
1 egg
½ teaspoon vanilla
1 jar Happy Birthday Cookie Mix

1. Preheat oven to 375°F. Line cookie sheets with parchment paper.

2. Beat butter in large bowl until fluffy. Beat in egg and vanilla. Add contents of jar to butter mixture. Beat 1 minute or until light dough forms.

3. Drop dough by rounded tablespoonfuls 2 inches apart onto prepared cookie sheets. Bake 10 minutes or until firm and golden brown. Let cookies stand 1 minute. Remove to wire racks to cool completely. *Makes 3 dozen cookies*

Happy Birthday Cookies

Granola Spice Muffin Mix

2¾ **cups all-purpose flour**
¾ **cup sugar**
⅔ **cup granola**
½ **cup raisins**
1 **tablespoon baking powder**
1 **teaspoon ground cinnamon**
½ **teaspoon salt**
¼ **teaspoon ground nutmeg**
⅛ **teaspoon ground allspice**

1. Layer ingredients in any order in 1-quart food storage jar with tight-fitting lid. Pack ingredients down tightly before adding another layer.

2. Seal jar. Cover top of jar with 8-inch circle of fabric, if desired; attach recipe gift tag with raffia or ribbon. *Makes one 1-quart jar*

Granola Spice Muffins

1 **jar Granola Spice Muffin Mix**
1½ **cups milk**
6 **tablespoons vegetable oil**
2 **eggs**
Coarse decorating sugar (optional)

1. Preheat oven to 400°F. Grease 18 standard (2½-inch) muffin pan cups. Place jar contents in large bowl. Mix milk, oil and eggs in small bowl until blended; stir into jar mixture just until moistened. Spoon into prepared muffin cups. Sprinkle with coarse sugar, if desired.

2. Bake 15 to 17 minutes or until toothpicks inserted into centers come out clean. Remove from pans; cool completely on wire racks. *Makes 18 muffins*

Crunchy Curried Snack Mix

2½ **cups rice cereal squares**
¾ **cup walnut halves**
¾ **cup dried cranberries or dried cherries**
2 **tablespoons brown sugar**
1½ **teaspoons curry powder**
¼ **teaspoon ground cumin**
¼ **teaspoon salt**

1. Layer 1¼ cups cereal, walnuts, cranberries and remaining 1¼ cups cereal in 2-quart food storage jar with tight-fitting lid. Combine brown sugar, curry powder, cumin and salt in small plastic food storage bag; close with twist tie. Cut off top of bag. Place bag on top of cereal.

2. Seal jar. Cover top of jar with 8-inch circle of fabric, if desired; attach recipe gift tag with raffia or ribbon. *Makes one 2-quart jar*

Crunchy Curried Snack Mix

1 **jar Crunchy Curried Snack Mix**
6 **tablespoons butter**

1. Preheat oven to 250°F. Remove seasoning packet from jar.

2. Melt butter in large skillet. Add contents of seasoning packet; mix well. Add remaining contents of jar; stir to coat. Spread mixture evenly on ungreased jelly-roll pan. Bake 40 to 45 minutes or until crisp, stirring every 15 minutes.

Makes 6 cups snack mix

Granola Spice Muffins

Irish Soda Bread Mix

2½ cups all-purpose flour
4 teaspoons baking powder
1 teaspoon salt
½ teaspoon baking soda
1¼ cups whole-wheat flour
¼ cup sugar
1 cup currants
2 teaspoons caraway seeds (optional)

1. Combine all-purpose flour, baking powder, salt and baking soda in large bowl. Layer flour mixture, whole wheat flour, sugar, currants and caraway seeds, if desired, in 1-quart food storage jar with tight-fitting lid. Pack ingredients down tightly before adding another layer.

2. Seal jar. Cover top of jar with 8-inch circle of fabric, if desired; attach recipe gift tag with raffia or ribbon. *Makes one 1-quart jar*

Irish Soda Bread

1 jar Irish Soda Bread Mix
½ cup (1 stick) butter, cut into small pieces
1⅓ to 1½ cups buttermilk

1. Preheat oven to 350°F. Grease large baking sheet.

2. Place contents of jar in large bowl. Cut in butter with pastry blender or two knives until mixture is crumbly. Add buttermilk; stir until slightly sticky dough forms.

3. Place dough on prepared baking sheet. Shape into 8-inch round. Bake 50 to 60 minutes or until bread is golden and crust is firm.

4. Cool bread on baking sheet 10 minutes. Carefully remove to wire rack to cool completely. Cut into wedges to serve. *Makes 12 servings*

Note: This bread tastes best the day it is made.

Irish Soda Bread

Sun-Dried Tomato Pesto

1 tablespoon vegetable oil
½ cup pine nuts
2 cloves garlic
1 jar (8 ounces) sun-dried tomatoes
    packed in oil, undrained
1 cup fresh Italian parsley
½ cup grated Parmesan cheese
¼ cup coarsely chopped pitted kalamata
    olives
2 teaspoons dried basil leaves
¼ teaspoon red pepper flakes

1. Heat oil in small skillet over medium-low heat. Add pine nuts; cook 30 to 45 seconds or until lightly browned, shaking pan constantly. Remove nuts from skillet with slotted spoon; drain on paper towels.

2. Combine toasted pine nuts and garlic in work bowl of food processor. Process using on/off pulsing action until mixture is finely chopped.

3. Add tomatoes with oil to work bowl; process until finely chopped. Add parsley, cheese, olives, basil and pepper flakes; process until mixture resembles thick paste, scraping down side of bowl occasionally with small spatula.

4. Spoon pesto into decorative food storage crock or jar with tight-fitting lid; cover.

5. Store in airtight container in refrigerator up to 1 month.   *Makes about 1½ cups pesto*

Serving Suggestion: For a quick and easy appetizer, serve this flavorful pesto spread on toasted slices of hearty Italian bread.

Wyoming Wild Barbecue Sauce

1 cup chili sauce
1 cup ketchup
¼ cup steak sauce
3 tablespoons dry mustard
2 tablespoons horseradish
2 tablespoons TABASCO® brand Pepper
    Sauce
1 tablespoon Worcestershire sauce
1 tablespoon finely chopped garlic
1 tablespoon dark molasses
1 tablespoon red wine vinegar

Combine ingredients in medium bowl. Whisk until sauce is well blended. Store in 1-quart covered jar in refrigerator up to 7 days. Use as a baste while grilling beef, chicken, pork or game.
Makes 3 cups sauce

Helpful Hint

Because its high sugar content can cause charring, barbecue sauce should be used during the last 10 to 30 minutes of cooking. Additional sauce may be served with the cooked meat, but for food safety, sauce leftover from brushing should not accompany the food after it is cooked.

Sun-Dried Tomato Pesto

Elegant Pecan Brandy Cake Mix

1¼ cups all-purpose flour
¾ cup packed brown sugar
1¼ cups granulated sugar
½ cup cornmeal
1 cup all-purpose flour
2 teaspoons baking powder
½ teaspoon salt
1 teaspoon ground cinnamon
¼ teaspoon ground nutmeg
1 cup coarsely chopped pecans, toasted*
1 cup powdered sugar

*Place nuts in microwavable dish. Microwave at HIGH 1 to 2 minutes or just until light golden brown, stirring nuts every 30 seconds. Let stand 3 minutes. Cool completely.

1. Layer all ingredients except powdered sugar in order listed above in 2-quart food storage jar with tight-fitting lid. Pack ingredients down lightly before adding another layer. Place powdered sugar in small plastic food storage bag; close with twist tie. Cut off top of bag. Place bag in jar.

2. Seal jar. Cover top of jar with 8-inch circle of fabric, if desired; attach recipe gift tag with raffia or ribbon.   *Makes one 2-quart jar*

Gift Idea: Assemble a gift basket with a jar of Pecan Brandy Cake Mix, a small bottle of brandy and a package of pecans. For a special gift, add a pretty bundt pan.

Elegant Pecan Brandy Cake

1 jar Elegant Pecan Brandy Cake Mix
1 cup (2 sticks) butter, softened
1 cup sour cream
5 eggs
½ cup plus 1 teaspoon brandy or rum
1 teaspoon vanilla
2 tablespoons butter
4 to 5 teaspoons milk

1. Preheat oven to 325°F. Generously grease and flour 10-inch Bundt or tube pan.

2. Remove powdered sugar packet from jar. Place remaining contents of jar in large bowl; stir until well blended. Beat 1 cup butter and sour cream in another large bowl until smooth. Beat in eggs, one at a time. Add ½ cup brandy and vanilla; beat until well blended. Gradually add flour mixture, beating until blended. Spread into prepared pan.

3. Bake 50 to 65 minutes or until toothpick inserted near center comes out clean. (Surface will appear slightly wet in center.) Cool cake in pan on wire rack 10 minutes. Loosen edges; remove cake from pan to wire rack. Cool completely.

4. Heat 2 tablespoons butter in medium saucepan over medium heat until melted and golden brown; cool slightly. Add powdered sugar, remaining 1 teaspoon brandy and enough milk to make pourable glaze; stir until smooth. Drizzle over cake.
  Makes 1 (10-inch) cake

Cocoa Brownies Mix

1¼ cups all-purpose flour
1 cup granulated sugar
¾ cup packed light brown sugar
⅔ cup unsweetened cocoa powder
½ cup chopped walnuts
1 teaspoon baking powder
¼ teaspoon salt

1. Layer ingredients in any order in 1-quart food storage jar with tight-fitting lid. Pack ingredients down lightly before adding another layer.

2. Seal jar. Cover top of jar with 8-inch circle of fabric, if desired; attach recipe gift tag with raffia or ribbon.

Makes one 1-quart jar

Cocoa Brownies

¾ cup (1½ sticks) butter, softened
3 eggs
1½ teaspoons vanilla
1 jar Cocoa Brownies Mix

1. Preheat oven to 350°F. Lightly grease 13×9-inch baking pan.

2. Beat butter in large bowl until smooth. Beat in eggs and vanilla until blended. (Mixture may appear curdled.) Add contents of jar to butter mixture; stir until well blended.

3. Spread batter evenly in prepared pan. Bake 20 to 25 minutes or until brownies spring back when lightly touched. Do not overbake. Cool in pan on wire rack.

Makes 2½ dozen brownies

Oatmeal-Chip Cookie Mix in a Jar

⅔ cup all-purpose flour
½ teaspoon baking soda
½ teaspoon ground cinnamon
¼ teaspoon salt
⅓ cup packed brown sugar
⅓ cup granulated sugar
¾ cup NESTLÉ® TOLL HOUSE® Semi-Sweet Chocolate or Butterscotch Flavored Morsels
1½ cups quick or old-fashioned oats
½ cup chopped nuts

COMBINE flour, baking soda, cinnamon and salt in small bowl. Place flour mixture in 1-quart jar. Layer remaining ingredients in order listed above, pressing lightly after each layer. Seal with lid and decorate with fabric and ribbon.

Recipe to Attach
BEAT ½ cup (1 stick) softened butter or margarine, 1 egg and ½ teaspoon vanilla extract in large mixer bowl until blended. Add cookie mix; mix well, breaking up any clumps. Drop by rounded tablespoon onto ungreased baking sheets. Bake in preheated 375°F. oven for 8 to 10 minutes. Cool on baking sheets for 2 minutes; remove to wire racks. Makes about 2 dozen cookies.

Italian Tomato and Pasta Soup Mix

2½ cups farfalle (bow tie) or rotini pasta
2 tablespoons dried vegetable flakes, soup greens or dehydrated vegetables
1 tablespoon dried minced onion
1 teaspoon chicken bouillon granules
1 teaspoon dried Italian seasoning
1 teaspoon sugar
½ teaspoon dried minced garlic
¼ teaspoon black pepper
½ cup grated Parmesan cheese

1. Place pasta in 1-quart food storage jar with tight-fitting lid. Add vegetable flakes, onion, bouillon granules, Italian seasoning, sugar, garlic and pepper. Shake jar to mix seasonings. Place Parmesan cheese in small plastic food storage bag; close with twist tie. Cut off top of bag. Place bag on top of pasta.

2. Seal jar. Cover top of jar with 8-inch circle of fabric, if desired; attach recipe gift tag with raffia or ribbon.   *Makes one 1-quart jar*

Note: Vegetable Flakes and Soup Greens made by McCORMICK® are available in the spice section of large supermarkets. If these products are not available, ask your grocer to order them. Also, look for dried vegetable flakes (bell peppers, carrots, etc.) in the bulk food section of specialty food markets such as natural or bulk food stores.

Italian Tomato and Pasta Soup

   1 jar Italian Tomato and Pasta Soup Mix
   5 cups water
   1 can (28 ounces) crushed tomatoes, undrained
   ½ package (10 ounces) frozen chopped spinach, thawed
   4 to 6 slices crisp-cooked bacon, crumbled

1. Remove cheese packet from jar; set aside.

2. Place water and remaining contents of jar in large saucepan. Bring to a boil over high heat; boil 10 to 12 minutes. Add tomatoes with juice, spinach and bacon; stir. Reduce heat; simmer 10 to 12 minutes or until pasta is tender. Serve with Parmesan cheese.
Makes 4 to 5 servings

Note: 3 cups chopped fresh spinach, rinsed and stemmed, can be substituted for frozen spinach.

Italian Tomato and Pasta Soup

Easy Cocoa Mix

2 cups nonfat dry milk powder
1 cup sugar
¾ cup powdered non-dairy creamer
½ cup unsweetened cocoa powder
¼ teaspoon salt

1. Combine all ingredients in medium bowl until well blended. Spoon into 1-quart food storage jar with tight-fitting lid.

2. Seal jar. Cover top of jar with 8-inch circle of fabric, if desired; attach serving instructions on gift tag with raffia or ribbon.

Makes about 4 cups mix or 16 servings

For single serving: Place rounded ¼ cup Easy Cocoa Mix in mug or cup; add ¾ cup boiling water. Stir until mix is dissolved. Top with sweetened whipped cream and marshmallows, if desired. Serve immediately.

Gift Idea: Assemble a gift basket with a jar of Easy Cocoa Mix, a package of miniature marshmallows and two extra-large mugs.

Mocha Coffee Mix

1 cup nonfat dry milk powder
¾ cup granulated sugar
⅔ cup powdered non-dairy creamer
½ cup unsweetened cocoa powder
⅓ cup instant coffee, pressed through fine sieve
¼ cup packed light brown sugar
1 teaspoon ground cinnamon
¼ teaspoon salt
¼ teaspoon ground nutmeg

1. Combine all ingredients in medium bowl until well blended. Spoon into 1-quart food storage jar with tight-fitting lid.

2. Seal jar. Cover top of jar with 8-inch circle of fabric, if desired; attach serving instructions on gift tag with raffia or ribbon.

Makes about 3½ cups mix or 10 to 12 servings

For single serving: Place rounded ¼ cup Mocha Coffee Mix in mug or cup; add ¾ cup boiling water. Stir until mix is dissolved. Serve immediately.

Left to right: Easy Cocoa and Mocha Coffee

Chocolate Cherry Pancake Mix

   2 cups all-purpose flour
   ⅓ cup sugar
  4½ teaspoons baking powder
   ½ teaspoon *each* baking soda and salt
   1 cup dried cherries
   ⅔ cup semisweet chocolate chips

1. Combine flour, sugar, baking powder, baking soda and salt in large bowl. Layer flour mixture and remaining ingredients in 1-quart food storage jar with tight-fitting lid. Pack ingredients down lightly before adding each layer.

2. Seal jar. Cover top of jar with 8-inch circle of fabric, if desired; attach recipe gift tag with raffia or ribbon.   *Makes one 1-quart jar*

Chocolate Cherry Pancakes

   2 eggs, beaten
   ¼ cup (½ stick) butter, melted
   1 jar Chocolate Cherry Pancake Mix
  1½ to 2 cups milk

1. Combine eggs and melted butter in large bowl. Add contents of jar; stir until blended. Add 1½ cups milk; stir until dry ingredients are moistened. Add additional milk for thinner pancakes.

2. Heat griddle or large nonstick skillet until a drop of water sizzles. Pour batter onto hot griddle ¼ cup at a time. Cook pancakes until golden on both sides.
   Makes 20 to 24 pancakes

Cocoa Raisin-Chip Cookie Mix

  1½ cups all-purpose flour
  1½ cups semisweet chocolate chips
   1 cup packed brown sugar
   1 cup raisins
   ¾ cup chopped walnuts
   ½ cup granulated sugar
   ¼ cup unsweetened cocoa powder
   1 teaspoon baking powder

1. Layer ingredients in any order in 1½-quart food storage jar with tight-fitting lid. Pack ingredients down tightly before adding another layer.

2. Seal jar. Cover top of jar with 8-inch circle of fabric, if desired; attach recipe gift tag with raffia or ribbon.   *Makes one 1½-quart jar*

Cocoa Raisin-Chip Cookies

   ½ cup (1 stick) butter, softened
   ½ cup shortening
   2 eggs
   1 teaspoon vanilla
   1 jar Cocoa Raisin-Chip Cookie Mix

1. Preheat oven to 350°F. Grease and flour cookie sheets. Beat butter and shortening in bowl. Beat in eggs, one at a time. Stir in vanilla. (Mixture may appear curdled.) Stir jar contents into butter mixture until well blended. Drop by tablespoonfuls onto prepared sheets.

2. Bake 10 to 12 minutes or until golden. Remove to wire racks to cool.   *Makes 4 dozen cookies*

Chocolate Cherry Pancakes

Taco Bean Chili Mix

½ cup dried kidney beans
½ cup dried pinto beans
½ cup dried red beans
1 package (1¼ ounces) taco seasoning mix
1 tablespoon dried minced onion
½ teaspoon chili powder or chipotle chili pepper seasoning
¼ teaspoon ground cumin
1½ cups tortilla chips, slightly crushed

1. Layer kidney beans, pinto beans and red beans in 1-quart food storage jar with tight-fitting lid. Combine taco seasoning mix, onion, chili powder and cumin in small plastic food storage bag; close with twist tie. Cut off top of bag. Place bag in jar spreading out to cover beans. Add tortilla chips.

2. Seal jar. Cover top of jar with 8-inch circle of fabric, if desired; attach recipe gift tag with raffia or ribbon.   *Makes one 1-quart jar*

Taco Bean Chili

1 jar Taco Bean Chili Mix
4 cups water
1 can (14½ ounces) diced tomatoes with green chilies, undrained
1 can (8 ounces) tomato sauce
1 pound ground beef or ground turkey, browned and drained
Shredded cheese, chopped lettuce, sliced black olives (optional)

1. Remove chips and seasoning packet from jar; set aside.

2. Place beans in large bowl; cover with water. Soak 6 to 8 hours or overnight. (To quick soak beans, place beans in large saucepan; cover with water. Bring to a boil over high heat. Boil 2 minutes. Remove from heat; let soak, covered, 1 hour.) Drain beans; discard water.

3. Place soaked beans, water, tomatoes with juice, tomato sauce, ground beef and contents of seasoning packet in Dutch oven. Bring to a boil over high heat. Cover; reduce heat and simmer 1½ to 2 hours or until beans are tender.

4. Crush tortilla chips. Stir into chili and cook 5 to 10 minutes to thicken. Serve with cheese, lettuce and olives, if desired.   *Makes 6 to 8 servings*

Taco Bean Chili

Classic Candy Creations

Nothing says "I love you"

quite like a box of candy—

especially when it's

homemade! With their

crunchy nuts, creamy

fillings and luscious

chocolate, these confections

are sure to dazzle friends

and family alike.

40

Reese's® Peanut Butter and Milk Chocolate Chip Mudd Balls

1¾ cups (11-ounce package) REESE'S® Peanut Butter and Milk Chocolate Chips, divided
½ teaspoon shortening (do not use butter, margarine, spread or oil)

1. Coarsely chop 1¼ cups chips in food processor or by hand; place in medium bowl.

2. Place remaining ½ cup chips and shortening in small microwave-safe bowl. Microwave at HIGH (100%) 45 seconds; stir. If necessary, microwave at HIGH an additional 15 seconds at a time, stirring after each heating, until chips are melted and mixture is smooth when stirred.

3. Pour melted chocolate mixture over chopped chips; stir to coat evenly. With hands, form mixture into 1-inch balls. Place in small candy cups, if desired. Store in cool, dry place.

Makes about 18 candies

Reese's® Peanut Butter and Milk Chocolate Chip Mudd Balls

Stuffed Pecans

½ cup semisweet chocolate chips
¼ cup sweetened condensed milk
½ teaspoon vanilla
½ cup powdered sugar
80 large pecan halves

1. Melt chips in small saucepan over very low heat, stirring constantly. Remove from heat. Stir in sweetened condensed milk and vanilla until smooth. Stir in powdered sugar to make stiff mixture. (If chocolate mixture is too soft, refrigerate until easier to handle.)

2. Place 1 rounded teaspoonful chocolate mixture on flat side of 1 pecan half. Top with another pecan half. Repeat with remaining chocolate mixture and pecans. Store in refrigerator. *Makes about 40 candies*

White Chocolate-Dipped Apricots

3 ounces white chocolate, coarsely chopped
20 dried apricot halves

1. Line baking sheet with waxed paper; set aside. Melt white chocolate in bowl over hot (not boiling) water, stirring constantly.

2. Dip half of each apricot piece in chocolate, coating both sides. Place on prepared baking sheet. Refrigerate until firm. Store in refrigerator in container between layers of waxed paper.
Makes 20 apricots

Helpful Hint

White chocolate is a combination of cocoa butter, sugar, milk solids, vanilla and emulsifiers. Some products labeled "white chocolate" do not contain cocoa butter. They are simply coatings, so when purchasing white chocolate, check the ingredient list for cocoa butter.

White Chocolate-Dipped Apricots and Stuffed Pecans

White Truffles

2 pounds vanilla-flavored candy coating*
1 (14-ounce) can EAGLE BRAND®
   Sweetened Condensed Milk
   (NOT evaporated milk)
1 tablespoon vanilla extract
1 pound chocolate-flavored candy
   coating,* melted, or unsweetened
   cocoa

Also known as confectioner's or summer coating.

1. In heavy saucepan, over low heat, melt vanilla candy coating with EAGLE BRAND®. Remove from heat; stir in vanilla. Cool.

2. Shape into 1-inch balls. With wooden pick, partially dip each ball into melted chocolate candy coating or roll in cocoa. Place on wax paper-lined baking sheets until firm. Store covered at room temperature or in refrigerator.

Makes about 8 dozen truffles

Flavoring Options: Amaretto: Omit vanilla. Add 3 tablespoons amaretto or other almond-flavored liqueur and ½ teaspoon almond extract. Roll in finely chopped toasted almonds. **Orange:** Omit vanilla. Add 3 tablespoons orange-flavored liqueur. Roll in finely chopped toasted almonds mixed with finely grated orange rind. **Rum:** Omit vanilla. Add ¼ cup dark rum. Roll in flaked coconut. **Bourbon:** Omit vanilla. Add 3 tablespoons bourbon. Roll in finely chopped toasted nuts.

Peppermint Chocolate Fudge

1 (12-ounce) package milk chocolate chips
   (2 cups)
1 cup (6 ounces) semi-sweet chocolate
   chips
1 (14-ounce) can EAGLE BRAND®
   Sweetened Condensed Milk
   (NOT evaporated milk)
   Dash salt
½ teaspoon peppermint extract
¼ cup crushed hard peppermint candy

1. In heavy saucepan over low heat, melt chips with EAGLE BRAND® and salt. Remove from heat; stir in peppermint extract. Spread evenly in foil-lined 8- or 9-inch square pan. Sprinkle with peppermint candy.

2. Chill 2 hours or until firm. Turn fudge onto cutting board; peel off foil and cut into squares. Store loosely covered at room temperature.

Makes about 2 pounds fudge

White Truffles

Peanut Butter Fudge

1 cup creamy peanut butter
1 cup sweetened condensed milk
1 cup powdered sugar
1 teaspoon vanilla
½ cup raisins, chopped

1. Butter 8-inch square pan; set aside.

2. Combine peanut butter, condensed milk, powdered sugar and vanilla in medium bowl. Beat with electric mixer until smooth. Stir in raisins. Press into prepared pan. Score fudge into squares with knife. Refrigerate until firm.

3. Cut into squares. Store in refrigerator.

Makes about 1½ pounds fudge

Helpful Hint

After opening, wrap raisins securely in plastic wrap or store them in an airtight container at room temperature. They will keep for several months. If refrigerated in a tightly covered container, raisins will keep for up to one year.

Tropical Sugarplums

½ cup white chocolate chips
¼ cup light corn syrup
½ cup chopped dates
¼ cup chopped maraschino cherries, well drained
1 teaspoon vanilla
¼ teaspoon rum extract
1¼ cups crushed gingersnaps
Flaked coconut

1. Combine white chocolate chips and corn syrup in large skillet. Cook and stir over low heat until melted and smooth.

2. Stir in dates, cherries, vanilla and rum extract until well blended. Add gingersnaps; stir until well blended. (Mixture will be stiff.)

3. Shape mixture into ¾-inch balls; roll in coconut. Place in miniature paper candy cups, if desired. Serve immediately or let stand overnight to allow flavors to blend.

Makes about 2 dozen candies

Tropical Sugarplums

Rocky Road Clusters

2 cups (12-ounce package) NESTLÉ® TOLL HOUSE® Semi-Sweet Chocolate Morsels
1 can (14 ounces) NESTLÉ® CARNATION® Sweetened Condensed Milk
2½ cups miniature marshmallows
1 cup coarsely chopped nuts
1 teaspoon vanilla extract

LINE baking sheets with waxed paper.

COMBINE morsels and sweetened condensed milk in large, uncovered, microwave-safe bowl. Microwave on HIGH (100%) power for 1 minute. STIR. Morsels may retain some of their original shape. If necessary, microwave at additional 10- to 15-second intervals, stirring just until morsels are melted. Stir in marshmallows, nuts and vanilla extract.

DROP by heaping tablespoon in mounds onto prepared baking sheets. Refrigerate until firm.

Makes about 2 dozen candies

Toasted Almond Bark

½ cup slivered almonds
12 ounces white chocolate, coarsely chopped
1 tablespoon shortening

1. Preheat oven to 325°F.

2. Spread almonds on baking sheet. Bake 12 minutes or until golden brown, stirring occasionally.

3. Meanwhile, butter another baking sheet. Spread warm almonds on buttered baking sheet.

4. Melt white chocolate with shortening in heavy, small saucepan over very low heat, stirring constantly. Spoon evenly over almonds, spreading about ¼ inch thick. Refrigerate until almost firm.

5. Cut into squares, but do not remove from baking sheet. Refrigerate until firm.

Makes about 1 pound bark

Excellent Mint Wafers

3½ to 4 cups powdered sugar
⅔ cup sweetened condensed milk
Food coloring, any color
½ teaspoon peppermint, spearmint or wintergreen extract

Line baking sheet with waxed paper. Combine 3½ cups powdered sugar and condensed milk in large bowl. Add food coloring, a few drops at a time, until desired color is reached. Knead in extract and enough powdered sugar until smooth, creamy texture is reached. Shape mixture into 1-inch balls. Place about 1 inch apart on baking sheet. Flatten each ball with fork to about ¼-inch thickness. Let stand, uncovered, at room temperature about 1 hour or until firm.   *Makes about 1 pound candy*

Fireballs

1 (12-ounce) package semisweet chocolate chips
¼ cup butter or margarine
½ cup walnuts, toasted and finely chopped
2 tablespoons dark rum
1½ teaspoons TABASCO® brand Pepper Sauce
⅓ cup granulated sugar

Melt chocolate and butter in small saucepan over very low heat. Stir in walnuts, rum and TABASCO® Sauce. Refrigerate about 15 minutes. Shape chocolate mixture into 1-inch balls; roll balls in granulated sugar to coat. Refrigerate until ready to serve.   *Makes about 34 balls*

Cashew Macadamia Crunch

2 cups (11.5-ounce package) HERSHEY'S Milk Chocolate Chips
¾ cup coarsely chopped salted or unsalted cashews
¾ cup coarsely chopped salted or unsalted macadamia nuts
½ cup (1 stick) butter, softened
½ cup sugar
2 tablespoons light corn syrup

1. Line 9-inch square pan with foil, extending foil over edges of pan. Butter foil. Cover bottom of prepared pan with chocolate chips.

2. Combine cashews, macadamia nuts, butter, sugar and corn syrup in large heavy skillet; cook over low heat, stirring constantly, until butter is melted and sugar is dissolved. Increase heat to medium; cook, stirring constantly, until mixture begins to cling together and turns medium golden brown (about 10 minutes).

3. Pour mixture over chocolate chips in pan, spreading evenly. Cool. Refrigerate until chocolate is firm. Remove from pan; peel off foil. Break into pieces. Store tightly covered in cool, dry place. *Makes about 1½ pounds candy*

Vanilla Caramels

1 cup sugar
1 (14-ounce) can EAGLE BRAND® Sweetened Condensed Milk (NOT evaporated milk)
Dash salt
1 tablespoon butter or margarine
½ teaspoon vanilla extract

1. Butter 8×8-inch square baking dish; set aside. Place sugar in heavy saucepan over low heat and stir constantly to prevent burning; stir until melted and the color of maple syrup. Gradually add EAGLE BRAND® and salt. Cook over low heat about 15 minutes (do not overcook). Remove from heat; add butter and vanilla. Immediately pour into prepared dish. Cool completely.

2. When caramel is completely cooled, remove from pan and cut into squares.
Makes 1¼ pounds candy

Cashew Macadamia Crunch

Coconut Balls

½ cup golden raisins, chopped
½ cup pitted prunes or dates, chopped
½ cup graham cracker crumbs
½ cup powdered sugar
1 tablespoon grated orange peel
½ cup sweetened condensed milk
1 cup shredded coconut

1. Combine raisins, prunes, graham cracker crumbs, sugar and orange peel in medium bowl. Stir in condensed milk. Refrigerate until firm enough to shape into balls, about 30 minutes.

2. Place coconut in shallow bowl.

3. For each candy, shape scant tablespoonful fruit mixture into 1-inch ball. Roll in coconut.

4. Store in refrigerator.   *Makes 30 candies*

Coconut Balls

Easy Luscious Fudge

2 cups (12 ounces) semisweet chocolate chips
¾ cup milk chocolate chips
2 squares (1 ounce each) unsweetened chocolate, coarsely chopped
1 can (14 ounces) sweetened condensed milk
1 cup miniature marshmallows
½ cup chopped walnuts (optional)

1. Line 8-inch square pan with foil, extending 1-inch over ends of pan. Lightly butter foil.

2. Melt chocolates in medium saucepan over low heat, stirring constantly. Remove from heat. Stir in condensed milk; add marshmallows and walnuts, if desired; stir until blended.

3. Spread chocolate mixture evenly in prepared pan. Score into 2-inch triangles by cutting halfway through fudge with sharp knife while fudge is still warm.

4. Refrigerate until firm. Remove from pan by lifting fudge and foil. Place on cutting board; cut along score lines into triangles. Remove foil. Store in airtight container in refrigerator.
Makes about 3 dozen pieces

Variation: For Mint Fudge, substitute 1⅔ cups (10 ounces) mint chocolate chips for semisweet chocolate chips and ½ cup chopped party mints for walnuts.

Easy Luscious Fudge

Butterscotch Rocky Road

1½ cups miniature marshmallows
1 cup coarsely chopped pecans
2 cups (12 ounces) butterscotch chips
½ cup sweetened condensed milk

1. Butter 13×9-inch pan. Spread marshmallows and pecans evenly on bottom of pan.

2. Melt butterscotch chips in heavy, medium saucepan over low heat, stirring constantly. Stir in condensed milk until smooth.

3. Pour butterscotch mixture over marshmallows and pecans, covering entire mixture. If necessary, use knife or small spatula to help cover marshmallows and nuts with butterscotch mixture. Let stand in pan until set.

4. Cut into squares. Store in refrigerator.

Makes about 1 pound candy

Helpful Hint

Warm nuts are easier to chop than cold or room temperature nuts. Place 1 cup of shelled nuts in a microwavable dish and heat at HIGH about 30 seconds or just until warm; chop as desired.

Cherry Almond Clusters

1 (8-ounce) package semisweet baking
** chocolate, coarsely chopped**
1 cup slivered almonds, toasted
1 cup dried tart cherries

Place chocolate in microwave-safe bowl. Microwave on HIGH (100% power) 2 minutes, stirring after 1 minute. Stir until chocolate is completely melted. Add almonds and dried cherries; mix until completely coated with chocolate. Drop by teaspoons onto waxed paper. Refrigerate until firm. *Makes 2 dozen candies*

Note: To toast almonds, spread almonds on ungreased baking sheet. Bake in preheated 350°F oven 5 to 7 minutes, stirring occasionally.

Favorite recipe from **Cherry Marketing Institute**

Mocha-Walnut Rum Balls

1 package (8½ ounces) chocolate wafer cookies
2 cups powdered sugar, divided
1¼ cups finely chopped toasted walnuts
2 tablespoons instant coffee granules
⅓ to ½ cup rum
2 tablespoons light corn syrup
½ teaspoon instant espresso coffee powder

Place cookies in food processor or blender; process until powdery crumbs form. Combine crumbs, 1½ cups powdered sugar and walnuts in large bowl. Dissolve coffee granules in ⅓ cup rum; stir in corn syrup. Blend rum mixture into crumb mixture until crumbs are moist enough to hold together. Add 2 to 3 tablespoons more rum, if necessary. Shape into 1-inch balls. Combine remaining ½ cup powdered sugar and espresso coffee powder in shallow bowl. Roll balls in sugar mixture to coat. Store loosely packed between sheets of waxed paper or foil in airtight container up to 2 weeks.

Makes about 100 balls

Peanutty Patties

MAZOLA NO STICK® Cooking Spray
1 cup sugar
1 cup KARO® Light Corn Syrup
1 cup creamy peanut butter
2 cups roasted peanuts

1. Spray large cookie sheets with cooking spray.

2. In large saucepan combine sugar and corn syrup. Bring to boil over medium heat; boil 1 minute. Remove from heat. Add peanut butter; stir until completely melted. Stir in peanuts.

3. Drop by tablespoonfuls onto prepared cookie sheets; cool until firm. Store covered in refrigerator in single layer.

Makes about 32 patties

Buckeye Balls

1½ cups JIF® Creamy Peanut Butter
½ cup butter or margarine, softened
1 teaspoon vanilla
½ teaspoon salt
3 to 4 cups confectioners' sugar
Coating
1 pound chocolate flavored candy coating
2 tablespoons CRISCO® all-vegetable shortening

1. Combine peanut butter, butter, vanilla and salt in large bowl. Beat at low speed of electric mixer until blended. Add 2 cups confectioners' sugar. Beat until blended. Continue adding sugar ½ cup at a time until mixture shaped into ball will hold together on toothpick. Shape into ¾-inch balls. Place on waxed paper-lined tray. Refrigerate.

2. For coating, combine candy coating and shortening in microwave-safe bowl. Microwave at 50% (MEDIUM) for 30 seconds. Stir. Repeat until mixture is smooth.

3. Insert toothpick into candy ball. Dip ¾ ball into melted coating. Scrape off excess. Place on waxed paper-lined tray. Remove toothpick. Smooth over holes. Refrigerate until coating is firm; remove from paper. Store at room temperature in covered container.

Makes 8 dozen candies

No-Cook Sour Cream Fondant

⅔ cup butter, softened
½ cup sour cream
1 teaspoon vanilla
½ teaspoon salt
2 packages (1 pound each) powdered sugar (about 8 cups), sifted and divided

1. Combine butter, sour cream, vanilla and salt in large bowl; beat with electric mixer at medium speed until smooth. Gradually add ½ of powdered sugar, beating well. Stir in enough remaining powdered sugar with wooden spoon to make mixture stiff.

2. Turn out powdered sugar mixture onto countertop or cutting board. Knead dough until smooth and pliable. Shape dough into balls or patties. Store in airtight container in refrigerator.

Makes about 10 dozen pieces (2½ pounds)

Variation: Immediately after shaping dough into balls or patties, roll in finely chopped honey-roasted cashews. You can also experiment with fondant to make different candies. Try adding flavored extracts, such as lemon, to taste. Or, roll fondant into balls; dip in melted chocolate.

Buckeye Balls

Double Peanut Clusters

**1⅔ cups (10-ounce package) REESE'S®
Peanut Butter Chips
1 tablespoon shortening (do not use
butter, margarine, spread or oil)
2 cups salted peanuts**

1. Line cookie sheet with wax paper.

2. Place peanut butter chips and shortening in large microwave-safe bowl. Microwave at HIGH (100%) 1½ minutes; stir until chips are melted and mixture is smooth. If necessary, microwave an additional 30 seconds until chips are melted when stirred. Stir in peanuts.

3. Drop by rounded teaspoons onto prepared cookie sheet. (Mixture may also be dropped into small paper candy cups.) Cool until set. Store in cool, dry place. *Makes about 2½ dozen clusters*

Butterscotch Nut Clusters: Follow above directions, substituting 1¾ cups (11-ounce package) HERSHEY'S Butterscotch Chips for Peanut Butter Chips.

Cookies 'n' Crème Fudge

**3 (6-ounce) packages white chocolate
baking squares
1 (14-ounce) can EAGLE BRAND®
Sweetened Condensed Milk
(NOT evaporated milk)
⅛ teaspoon salt
2 cups coarsely crushed chocolate crème-
filled sandwich cookies (about
20 cookies)**

1. Line 8-inch square baking pan with waxed paper. In heavy saucepan over low heat, melt white chocolate with EAGLE BRAND® and salt. Remove from heat. Stir in crushed cookies. Spread evenly in prepared pan. Chill 2 hours or until firm.

2. Turn fudge onto cutting board. Peel off paper; cut into squares. Store tightly covered at room temperature. · *Makes about 2½ pounds fudge*

Double Peanut Clusters

Cookies 'n' Crème Fudge

Chocolate Mint Truffles

**1¾ cups (11.5-ounce package) NESTLÉ®
TOLL HOUSE® Milk Chocolate Morsels
1 cup (6 ounces) NESTLÉ® TOLL HOUSE®
Semi-Sweet Chocolate Morsels
¾ cup heavy whipping cream
1 tablespoon peppermint extract
1½ cups finely chopped walnuts, toasted, or
NESTLÉ® TOLL HOUSE® Baking Cocoa**

LINE baking sheet with wax paper.

PLACE milk chocolate and semi-sweet morsels in large mixer bowl. Heat cream to a gentle boil in small saucepan; pour over morsels. Let stand for 1 minute; stir until smooth. Stir in peppermint extract. Cover with plastic wrap; refrigerate for 35 to 45 minutes or until slightly thickened. Stir just until color lightens slightly. (*Do not* overmix or truffles will be grainy.)

DROP by rounded teaspoonful onto prepared baking sheet; refrigerate for 10 to 15 minutes. Shape into balls; roll in walnuts or cocoa. Store in airtight container in refrigerator.

Makes about 48 truffles

Variation: After rolling chocolate mixture into balls, freeze for 30 to 40 minutes. Microwave 1¾ cups (11.5-ounce package) NESTLÉ® TOLL HOUSE® Milk Chocolate Morsels and 3 tablespoons vegetable shortening in medium, uncovered, microwave-safe bowl on MEDIUM-HIGH (70%) power for 1 minute. STIR. Morsels may retain some of their original shape. If necessary, microwave at additional 10- to 15-second intervals, stirring just until morsels are melted. Dip truffles into chocolate mixture; shake off excess. Place on foil-lined baking sheets. Refrigerate for 15 to 20 minutes or until set. Store in airtight container in refrigerator.

Luscious Chocolate Covered Strawberries

**3 squares (1 ounce each) semi-sweet
chocolate
2 tablespoons I CAN'T BELIEVE IT'S NOT
BUTTER!® Spread
1 tablespoon coffee liqueur (optional)
6 to 8 large strawberries with stems**

In small microwave-safe bowl, microwave chocolate and I Can't Believe It's Not Butter!® Spread at HIGH (Full Power) 1 minute or until chocolate is melted; stir until smooth. Stir in liqueur. Dip strawberries in chocolate mixture, then refrigerate on waxed paper-lined baking sheet until chocolate is set, at least 1 hour.

Makes 6 to 8 strawberries

Chocolate Mint Truffles

Chocolate-Nut Squares

**1 cup (6 ounces) semisweet chocolate
   chips
1 cup milk chocolate chips
1 tablespoon shortening
1 package (14 ounces) caramels
3 tablespoons milk
2 tablespoons butter or margarine
2 cups coarsely chopped pecans**

1. Line 8-inch square pan with buttered foil; set aside. Melt both kinds of chips with shortening in heavy small saucepan over very low heat, stirring constantly. Spoon half the chocolate mixture into prepared pan, spreading evenly over bottom and ¼ inch up sides of pan. Refrigerate until firm.

2. Meanwhile, combine caramels, milk and butter in heavy medium saucepan. Cook over medium heat, stirring constantly until smooth. Stir in pecans. Cool to lukewarm. Spread caramel mixture evenly over chocolate in pan. Melt remaining chocolate mixture again over very low heat, stirring constantly; spread over caramel layer. Refrigerate until almost firm. Cut into squares. Store in refrigerator.

Makes about 2 pounds candy

Tip: Squares are easier to cut without breaking if chocolate is not completely firm.

Chocolate Peppermints

**1 cup (6 ounces) semisweet chocolate
   chips
1 cup milk chocolate chips
¼ teaspoon peppermint extract
½ cup crushed peppermint candy**

Line baking sheet with buttered waxed paper; set aside. Melt both kinds of chips in heavy medium saucepan over very low heat, stirring constantly. Stir in peppermint extract. Spread mixture in rectangle about ¼ inch thick on prepared baking sheet. Sprinkle with candy; press into chocolate. Refrigerate until almost firm. Cut into squares. Refrigerate until firm before removing from paper.

Makes about 100 candies

Alternating from top: Chocolate Peppermints and Chocolate-Nut Squares

Rich Cocoa Balls

4 cups (about 1 pound) powdered sugar, divided
¾ cup HERSHEY'S Cocoa
1 can (14 ounces) sweetened condensed milk (not evaporated milk)
1 tablespoon vanilla extract
2 cups finely chopped nuts

1. Reserve ½ cup powdered sugar for coating. Stir together remaining 3½ cups powdered sugar and cocoa in large bowl. Add sweetened condensed milk and vanilla. Beat on medium speed of mixer until blended, about 2 minutes. Stir in nuts. Cover; refrigerate 30 minutes or until mixture is firm enough to handle.

2. Shape into 1-inch balls; roll in reserved ½ cup powdered sugar. Cover; refrigerate 2 hours or until firm. Store in refrigerator in tightly covered container.   *Makes about 5 dozen pieces*

Rich Minty Cocoa Balls: Omit nuts. Substitute ½ teaspoon peppermint extract for 1 tablespoon vanilla extract. Roll in crushed peppermint stick candy to coat.

Chocolate Raspberry Truffles

1 (14-ounce) can EAGLE BRAND® Sweetened Condensed Milk (NOT evaporated milk)
¼ cup raspberry liqueur
2 tablespoons butter or margarine
2 tablespoons seedless raspberry jam
2 (12-ounce) packages semi-sweet chocolate chips
½ cup powdered sugar or ground toasted almonds

1. In large microwave-safe bowl, combine EAGLE BRAND®, liqueur, butter and jam. Microwave at HIGH (100% power) 3 minutes.

2. Stir in chips until smooth. Cover and chill 1 hour.

3. Shape mixture into 1-inch balls and roll in powdered sugar or almonds. Store covered at room temperature.   *Makes 4 dozen truffles*

Buttery Peppermints

20 hard peppermint candies
5½ cups powdered sugar, divided
⅓ cup evaporated milk
¼ cup butter

1. Place peppermint candies and ½ cup powdered sugar in food processor; process using on/off pulsing action until consistency of powder.

2. Cook and stir evaporated milk, butter and ½ cup powdered candy mixture in heavy large saucepan over medium-low heat until candy dissolves and mixture just begins to boil. Transfer to large bowl.

3. Stir 4 cups powdered sugar into milk mixture with wooden spoon until well blended. Stir in additional powdered sugar, ¼ cup at a time, until consistency of dough. Place on surface lightly dusted with powdered sugar.

4. Knead dough until smooth. Divide dough into 4 equal portions.

5. Shape each portion into 20-inch-long roll. Cut each roll into ¾-inch pieces. Roll in remaining powdered candy mixture to coat.

6. For soft mints, store in airtight container at room temperature. For dry mints, keep uncovered several hours before storing in airtight container. *Makes about 8 dozen mints*

Chocolate Snowswirl Fudge

3 cups (18 ounces) semi-sweet chocolate
**   chips**
1 (14-ounce) can EAGLE BRAND®
**   Sweetened Condensed Milk**
**   (NOT evaporated milk)**
4 tablespoons butter or margarine, divided
1½ teaspoons vanilla extract
**   Dash salt**
1 cup chopped nuts
2 cups miniature marshmallows

1. In heavy saucepan over low heat, melt chips with EAGLE BRAND®, 2 tablespoons butter, vanilla and salt. Remove from heat; stir in nuts. Spread evenly in foil-lined 8- or 9-inch square pan.

2. In medium saucepan over low heat, melt marshmallows with remaining 2 tablespoons butter. Spread on top of fudge. With table knife or metal spatula, swirl top of fudge.

3. Chill at least 2 hours or until firm. Turn fudge onto cutting board; peel off foil and cut into squares. Store loosely covered at room temperature. *Makes about 2 pounds fudge*

Reese's® Peanut Butter and Milk Chocolate Chip Fudge

1½ cups sugar
⅔ cup (5-ounce can) evaporated milk
2 tablespoons butter
1½ cups miniature marshmallows
1¾ cups (11-ounce package) REESE'S®
   Peanut Butter and Milk Chocolate
   Chips
1 teaspoon vanilla extract

1. Line 8×8×2-inch baking pan with foil. Butter foil. Set aside.

2. Combine sugar, evaporated milk and butter in heavy medium saucepan. Cook over medium heat, stirring constantly, to a full rolling boil. Boil, stirring constantly, 5 minutes. Remove from heat; stir in marshmallows, chips and vanilla. Stir until marshmallows are melted. Pour into prepared pan. Refrigerate 1 hour or until firm. Cut into shapes with cookie cutters or cut into squares. Store tightly covered in a cool, dry place.
Makes about 1¾ pounds fudge

Honey Fruit Truffles

6 ounces unsweetened chocolate, finely
   chopped
½ cup honey
2 tablespoons butter or margarine
2 tablespoons heavy cream
½ cup chopped dried apricots
½ cup unsweetened cocoa powder

Combine chocolate, honey, butter and cream in top of double boiler. Cook over medium heat, stirring constantly, until chocolate is melted and smooth. Stir in apricots. Refrigerate 1 hour, or until mixture is firm. Form into ¾-inch balls; roll in cocoa powder. Store in airtight container until ready to serve.
Makes about 12 truffles

Microwave Directions: In medium, microwave-safe container, combine chocolate, honey, butter and cream. Microwave on HIGH (100%) for 1 minute; stir until smooth. Stir in apricots and proceed as directed.

Favorite recipe from **National Honey Board**

Reese's® Peanut Butter and Milk Chocolate Chip Fudge

Sweet & Savory Snacks

Delight family and friends with a gift straight from your kitchen! These snack mixes, popcorn treats and seasoned nuts will tame the munchies and win rave reviews. Salty, sweet, crunchy, chewy—there's something for everyone!

S'Mores on a Stick

1 (14-ounce) can EAGLE BRAND® Sweetened Condensed Milk (NOT evaporated milk), divided
1½ cups milk chocolate chips, divided
1 cup miniature marshmallows
11 whole graham crackers, halved crosswise
Toppings: chopped peanuts, mini candy-coated chocolate pieces, sprinkles

1. Microwave half of EAGLE BRAND® in microwave-safe bowl at HIGH (100% power) 1½ minutes. Stir in 1 cup chips until smooth; stir in marshmallows.

2. Spread chocolate mixture evenly by heaping tablespoonfuls onto 11 graham cracker halves. Top with remaining graham cracker halves; place on waxed paper.

3. Microwave remaining EAGLE BRAND® at HIGH (100% power) 1½ minutes; stir in remaining ½ cup chips, stirring until smooth. Drizzle mixture over cookies and sprinkle with desired toppings.

4. Let stand for 2 hours; insert a wooden craft stick into center of each cookie.

Makes 11 servings

S'Mores on a Stick

Praline Pecans & Cranberries

3½ cups pecan halves
¼ cup light corn syrup
¼ cup packed light brown sugar
2 tablespoons butter or margarine
1 teaspoon vanilla
¼ teaspoon baking soda
1½ cups dried cranberries or cherries

1. Preheat oven to 250°F. Cover large baking sheet with heavy-duty foil; set aside.

2. Grease 13×9-inch baking pan. Spread pecans in single layer in prepared pan.

3. Combine corn syrup, brown sugar and butter in medium microwavable bowl. Microwave at HIGH 1 minute; stir. Microwave 30 seconds to 1 minute or until boiling rapidly. Carefully stir in vanilla and baking soda until well blended. Drizzle evenly over pecans; stir until evenly coated.

4. Bake 1 hour, stirring every 20 minutes with wooden spoon. Immediately transfer mixture to prepared baking sheet, spreading pecans evenly over foil with lightly greased spatula. Cool completely.

5. Break pecans apart with wooden spoon. Combine pecans and cranberries in large bowl. Store in airtight container at room temperature up to 2 weeks. *Makes about 5 cups snack mix*

Spicy Sweet Popcorn

¼ cup popcorn kernels
1 tablespoon granulated sugar
1 teaspoon chili powder
½ teaspoon cinnamon
¼ teaspoon salt
Dash cayenne pepper
Vegetable cooking spray

Pop popcorn. Mix dry ingredients in large resealable plastic food storage bag. Add popcorn and spray with cooking spray. Close bag and mix. Repeat with cooking spray until popcorn is coated. *Makes about 6 cups popcorn*

Favorite recipe from **The Sugar Association, Inc.**

Helpful Hint

Like most spices, ground cinnamon will lose its strength over time, so if yours has been in the cabinet for a while, sniff or taste it before using to make sure it is still flavorful.

Praline Pecans & Cranberries

Reese's® Peanut Butter and Milk Chocolate Chip Cattails

**1¾ cups (11-ounce package) REESE'S®
    Peanut Butter and Milk Chocolate
    Chips, divided
  2 teaspoons shortening (do not use butter,
    margarine, spread or oil)
  12 to 14 pretzel rods**

1. Place sheet of wax paper on tray or counter top. Finely chop ¾ cup chips in food processor or by hand; place on wax paper. Line another tray or cookie sheet with wax paper.

2. Place remaining 1 cup chips and shortening in narrow deep microwave-safe bowl. Microwave at MEDIUM (50%) 1 minute; stir. If necessary, microwave additional 30 seconds at a time, stirring after each heating, until chips are melted and mixture is smooth when stirred.

3. Spoon chocolate over about ¾ of each pretzel rod; gently shake off excess. Holding pretzel by uncoated end, roll in chopped chips, pressing chips into chocolate. Place on prepared tray. Refrigerate 30 minutes or until set. Store coated pretzels in cool, dry place.

Makes 12 to 14 coated pretzels

Variation: Melt entire package of chips with 4 teaspoons shortening and dip small pretzels into mixture.

Fiery Garlic Bagel Thins

** 5 bagels
  ½ cup (1 stick) butter
  6 cloves garlic, minced
  2 tablespoons lemon juice
  ½ teaspoon TABASCO® brand Pepper
    Sauce
  Salt to taste**

Preheat broiler. Slice bagels crosswise into fifths. Melt butter in small saucepan. Add garlic; cook over low heat for 2 minutes or until garlic has softened. Add lemon juice, TABASCO® Sauce and salt. Liberally brush one side of each bagel slice with lemon-garlic butter. Broil bagels on one side about 1 minute until golden, watching carefully. Turn bagels over and broil until golden. Serve hot or store in an airtight container.

Makes 25 bagel thins

Reese's® Peanut Butter and Milk Chocolate Chip Cattails

Sesame Tortilla Crackers

2 tablespoons olive oil
1 tablespoon sesame seeds
¼ teaspoon onion powder
6 flour tortillas (6 inches in diameter)

1. Preheat oven to 450°F. Combine olive oil, sesame seeds and onion powder in small bowl. Brush oil mixture on one side of each tortilla, stacking tortillas oiled side up.

2. Cut tortilla stack into 6 wedges using sharp knife. Arrange wedges, oiled side up, in single layer on ungreased baking sheets.

3. Bake 6 to 8 minutes until crackers are golden brown. Transfer crackers to wire racks; cool completely. Store crackers in airtight container up to 3 days.   *Makes 36 crackers*

Hotsy Totsy Spiced Nuts

1 can (12 ounces) mixed nuts
3 tablespoons *Frank's® RedHot®* Original Cayenne Pepper Sauce
1 tablespoon vegetable oil
¾ teaspoon seasoned salt
¾ teaspoon garlic powder

1. Preheat oven to 250°F. Place nuts in 10×15-inch jelly-roll pan. Combine remaining ingredients in small bowl; pour over nuts. Toss to coat evenly.

2. Bake 45 minutes or until nuts are toasted and dry, stirring every 15 minutes. Cool completely.
Makes about 2 cups nut mix

Zesty Party Snack Mix

4 cups oven-toasted corn cereal squares
2 cans (1½ ounces each) *French's®* Potato Sticks
1 cup honey-roasted peanuts
3 tablespoons melted butter or oil
2 tablespoons *French's®* Worcestershire Sauce
2 tablespoons *Frank's® RedHot®* Original Cayenne Pepper Sauce
½ teaspoon seasoned salt

1. Combine cereal, potato sticks and peanuts in 3-quart microwavable bowl. Combine melted butter, Worcestershire, **Frank's RedHot** Sauce and seasoned salt in bowl; mix well. Pour butter mixture over cereal mixture. Toss to coat evenly.

2. Microwave, uncovered, on HIGH 6 minutes, stirring well every 2 minutes. Transfer to paper towels; cool completely.
Makes about 6 cups snack mix

Tex-Mex Snack Mix: Add 1 teaspoon each chili powder and ground cumin to butter mixture. Substitute 1 cup regular peanuts for honey-roasted nuts. Prepare as directed.

Italian Snack Mix: Add 1½ teaspoons Italian seasoning and ½ teaspoon garlic powder to butter mixture. Substitute ½ cup grated Parmesan cheese and ½ cup sliced almonds for honey-roasted nuts. Prepare as directed.

Indian Snack Mix: Omit seasoned salt. Add 2 teaspoons each sesame seeds and curry powder and ¼ teaspoon garlic salt to butter mixture. Substitute 1 cup cashews for honey-roasted nuts. Prepare as directed.

Top to bottom: Hotsy Totsy Spiced Nuts and Zesty Party Snack Mix

Spicy, Fruity Popcorn Mix

4 cups lightly salted popped popcorn
2 cups corn cereal squares
1½ cups dried pineapple wedges
1 package (6 ounces) dried fruit bits
   Butter-flavored nonstick cooking spray
2 tablespoons sugar
1 tablespoon ground cinnamon
1 cup yogurt-covered raisins

1. Preheat oven to 350°F. Combine popcorn, cereal, pineapple and fruit bits in large bowl; mix lightly. Transfer to 15×10-inch jelly-roll pan. Spray mixture generously with cooking spray.

2. Combine sugar and cinnamon in small bowl. Sprinkle ½ of the sugar mixture over popcorn mixture; toss lightly to coat. Spray mixture again with additional cooking spray. Add remaining sugar mixture; mix lightly.

3. Bake 10 minutes, stirring after 5 minutes. Cool completely in pan on wire rack. Add raisins; mix lightly. *Makes 8½ cups snack mix*

Nutty Onion Snack Mix

1 can (6 ounces) *French's*® French Fried
   Onions
2 cups mixed nuts
1½ cups small pretzel twists
2 cans (1½ ounces each) *French's*® Potato
   Sticks
3 tablespoons butter or margarine, melted
3 tablespoons *French's*® Bold n' Spicy
   Brown Mustard

1. Place French Fried Onions, nuts, pretzels and potato sticks in 4-quart microwave-safe bowl. Combine butter and mustard. Pour over mixture in bowl; toss well to coat evenly.

2. Microwave, uncovered, on HIGH for 6 minutes, stirring well every 2 minutes. Transfer to paper towels; cool completely.

Makes about 9 cups snack mix

Spicy, Fruity Popcorn Mix

Hershey's Easy Chocolate Cracker Snacks

**1⅔ cups (10-ounce package) HERSHEY'S
    Mint Chocolate Chips***
**2 cups (12-ounce package) HERSHEY'S
    Semi-Sweet Chocolate Chips**
**2 tablespoons shortening (do not use
    butter, margarine, spread or oil)**
**60 to 70 round buttery crackers (about
    one-half 1-pound box)**

**2 cups (11.5-ounce package) HERSHEY'S Milk Chocolate Chips
and ¼ teaspoon pure peppermint extract can be substituted for
mint chocolate chips.*

1. Line several trays or cookie sheets with wax
paper.

2. Place mint chocolate chips, chocolate chips
and shortening in large microwave-safe bowl.
Microwave at HIGH (100%) 1 minute; stir.
Continue heating 30 seconds at a time, stirring
after each heating, until chips are melted and
mixture is smooth when stirred.

3. Drop crackers into chocolate mixture one at a
time. Using tongs, push cracker into chocolate
so that it is covered completely. (If chocolate
begins to thicken, reheat 10 to 20 seconds in
microwave.) Remove from chocolate, tapping
lightly on edge of bowl to remove excess
chocolate. Place on prepared tray. Refrigerate
until chocolate hardens, about 20 minutes. For
best results, store tightly covered in refrigerator.
Makes about 5½ dozen crackers

Peanut Butter and Milk Chocolate: Use
1⅔ cups (10-ounce package) REESE'S® Peanut
Butter Chips, 2 cups (11.5-ounce package)
HERSHEY'S Milk Chocolate Chips and
2 tablespoons shortening. Proceed as directed.

Chocolate Raspberry: Use 1⅔ cups
(10-ounce package) HERSHEY'S Raspberry
Chips, 2 cups (11.5-ounce package) HERSHEY'S
Milk Chocolate Chips and 2 tablespoons
shortening. Proceed as directed.

White Chip and Toffee: Melt 2 bags
(12 ounces each) HERSHEY'S Premier White
Chips and 2 tablespoons shortening. Dip
crackers; before coating hardens sprinkle with
HEATH® BITS 'O BRICKLE® Toffee Bits.

Hershey₂s Easy Chocolate Cracker Snacks

Rosemary-Scented Nut Mix

2 tablespoons unsalted butter
2 cups pecan halves
1 cup unsalted macadamia nuts
1 cup walnuts
1 teaspoon dried rosemary, crushed
½ teaspoon salt
¼ teaspoon red pepper flakes

1. Preheat oven to 300°F. Melt butter in large saucepan over low heat. Add pecans, macadamia nuts and walnuts; mix well. Add rosemary, salt and red pepper flakes; cook and stir about 1 minute.

2. Spread mixture on ungreased nonstick baking sheet. Bake 15 minutes, stirring mixture occasionally. Cool completely in pan on wire rack.   *Makes about 4 cups mix*

Rosemary-Scented Nut Mix

Festive Caramel Apples

5 medium apples
5 wooden craft sticks
¾ cup chopped walnuts or pecans
1 package (14 ounces) caramels, unwrapped
1 tablespoon water
1 cup (6 ounces) semisweet chocolate chips
1 teaspoon shortening

1. Spray baking sheet with nonstick cooking spray; set aside. Wash and dry apples; insert wooden sticks into stem ends. Place nuts in shallow dish.

2. Combine caramels and water in small saucepan. Cook over medium heat, stirring constantly, until caramels are melted.

3. Dip apples, 1 at a time, into caramel mixture, turning to cover completely. Remove excess caramel mixture by scraping apple bottoms across rim of saucepan. Roll bottom half of apples in walnuts. Place on prepared baking sheet. Refrigerate at least 15 minutes.

4. Place chocolate and shortening in small microwavable bowl. Microwave at HIGH 1 to 2 minutes; stir until chips are melted. Drizzle chocolate decoratively over apples. Refrigerate 10 minutes or until chocolate is firm. Wrap apples individually; store in refrigerator.
                                                        Makes 5 apples

Festive Caramel Apples

Indian-Spiced Walnuts

2 egg whites, lightly beaten
1 tablespoon ground cumin
1½ teaspoons curry powder
1½ teaspoons salt
½ teaspoon sugar
4 cups California walnuts, halves and pieces

Preheat oven to 350°F. Coat large, shallow baking pan with nonstick cooking spray. In large bowl, mix egg whites with spices, salt and sugar. Stir in walnuts and coat thoroughly. Spread in prepared pan. Bake 15 to 18 minutes or until dry and crisp. Cool completely before serving. *Makes 4 cups nuts*

Favorite recipe from **Walnut Marketing Board**

Helpful Hint

Eggs separate more easily when cold. To separate a yolk from a white, gently break the egg in half over a small bowl. Holding a shell half in each hand, transfer the yolk back and forth between the two shell halves, allowing the white to drip into the bowl. Place the yolk into another bowl.

Seasoned Snack Mix

⅔ Butter Flavor CRISCO® Stick or ⅔ cup Butter Flavor CRISCO® all-vegetable shortening
¾ cup grated Parmesan cheese
2 teaspoons Worcestershire sauce
2 teaspoons Italian seasoning
¾ teaspoon garlic salt
¼ teaspoon onion powder
¼ teaspoon cayenne pepper
3 cups bite-size rice squares cereal
2 cups round toasted oat cereal
2 cups oyster crackers
2 cups pretzel sticks
1 can (7 ounces) Spanish peanuts
Salt, to taste

1. Preheat oven to 325°F. In Dutch oven melt ⅔ cup shortening. Remove from heat.

2. Stir in Parmesan cheese, Worcestershire sauce, Italian seasoning, garlic salt, onion powder and cayenne pepper.

3. Add rice squares and toasted oat cereal, oyster crackers, pretzel sticks and peanuts. Toss to coat. Spread on 12×17½×1-inch jelly-roll pan.

4. Bake at 325°F for 15 to 18 minutes or until toasted and golden brown, stirring once after 10 minutes. Cool. Store in covered container.
Makes 10 cups snack mix

Celestial Crackers

1 cup all-purpose flour
½ teaspoon baking powder
½ teaspoon paprika
¼ teaspoon salt
⅓ cup plus 1 tablespoon water, divided
3 tablespoons vegetable oil
1 egg white
  Toppings: sesame seeds, poppy seeds,
  garlic salt or dried herbs

1. Combine flour, baking powder, paprika and salt in medium bowl. Stir in ⅓ cup water and oil to form smooth dough.

2. Preheat oven to 400°F. Grease baking sheets.

3. Roll dough on floured surface to 14×12-inch rectangle. Cut dough into star and moon shapes using 2-inch cookie cutters. Place on prepared baking sheets.

4. Combine egg white and 1 tablespoon water; brush on crackers. Sprinkle with toppings as desired.

5. Bake 8 to 10 minutes or until edges begin to brown. Remove to wire racks; cool completely.

Makes 2½ dozen crackers

White Chocolate Pecan Corn

1 pop & serve bag (3.5 ounces) JOLLY
  TIME® Butter-Licious or Crispy 'n White
  Microwave Pop Corn, popped
8 ounces vanilla flavored candy coating
  (white chocolate) *or* 1 package
  (10 ounces) large vanilla flavored
  baking chips
½ cup pecan halves

Place popped pop corn in large bowl. Place candy coating in 1-quart glass measuring cup. Microwave on HIGH 1 to 1½ minutes, or until candy coating is shiny; stir to melt completely. Stir in pecans. Add mixture to pop corn and mix well. Spread on cookie sheet; allow to cool completely. *Makes about 2 quarts pop corn*

Note: One pop & serve (3.5-ounce) package JOLLY TIME® Microwave Pop Corn yields about 12 cups popped pop corn.

Cinnamon Apple Chips

2 cups unsweetened apple juice
1 cinnamon stick
2 Washington Red Delicious apples

1. In large skillet or saucepan, combine apple juice and cinnamon stick; bring to a low boil while preparing apples.

2. With paring knife, slice off ½ inch from tops and bottoms of apples and discard (or eat). Stand apples on either cut end; cut crosswise into ⅛-inch-thick slices, rotating apple as necessary to cut even slices.

3. Drop slices into boiling juice; cook 4 to 5 minutes or until slices appear translucent and lightly golden. Meanwhile, preheat oven to 250°F.

4. With slotted spatula, remove apple slices from juice and pat dry. Arrange slices on wire racks, making sure none overlap. Place racks on middle shelf in oven; bake 30 to 40 minutes until slices are lightly browned and almost dry to touch. Let chips cool on racks completely before storing in airtight container.

Makes about 40 chips

Tip: There is no need to core apples because boiling in juice for several minutes softens core and removes seeds.

Favorite recipe from **Washington Apple Commission**

Fiesta Party Mix

1 package (1.48 ounces) LAWRY'S® Spices & Seasonings for Chili
½ cup butter or margarine, melted
2 cups crispy wheat squares cereal
2 cups crispy corn squares cereal
1 box (10 ounces) bite-size cheese crackers
1 can (10 ounces to 11.5 ounces) mixed nuts
1 cup small twist pretzels

In small bowl combine Spices & Seasonings for Chili and butter; whisk until smooth. In extra large Ziploc® bag, combine cereal, crackers, nuts, and pretzels; shake together. Pour chili sauce over cereal mixture. Seal bag and gently toss cereal mixture until well coated. Spread mixture evenly over foil-lined baking sheet or bottom of broiler pan. Bake in preheated 300°F oven for 15 minutes, stirring occasionally. Serve warm or cool completely and store in airtight container until ready to serve.

Makes about 10 cups snack mix

Note: Do not use spread or tub butter/margarine products in this recipe.

Cinnamon Apple Chips

Cranberry-Orange Snack Mix

2 cups oatmeal cereal squares
2 cups corn cereal squares
2 cups mini pretzels
1 cup whole almonds
¼ cup butter
⅓ cup frozen orange juice concentrate, thawed
3 tablespoons packed brown sugar
1 teaspoon ground cinnamon
¾ teaspoon ground ginger
¼ teaspoon ground nutmeg
⅔ cup dried cranberries or raisins

1. Preheat oven to 250°F. Spray 13×9-inch baking pan with nonstick cooking spray.

2. Combine cereal squares, pretzels and almonds in large bowl; set aside.

3. Melt butter in medium microwavable bowl at HIGH 45 to 60 seconds. Stir in orange juice concentrate, brown sugar, cinnamon, ginger and nutmeg until blended. Pour over cereal mixture; stir well to coat. Spread in single layer in prepared pan.

4. Bake 50 minutes, stirring every 10 minutes. Stir in cranberries. Let cool in pan on wire rack, leaving uncovered until mixture is crisp. Store in airtight container or resealable plastic food storage bags. *Makes 8 cups snack mix*

Rocky Road Popcorn Balls

6 cups unbuttered popped popcorn, lightly salted
2 cups "M&M's"® Chocolate Mini Baking Bits, divided
1¾ cups peanuts
¼ cup (½ stick) butter
4 cups miniature marshmallows

In large bowl combine popcorn, 1½ cups "M&M's"® Chocolate Mini Baking Bits and peanuts; set aside. Place remaining ½ cup "M&M's"® Chocolate Mini Baking Bits in shallow bowl; set aside. In large saucepan over low heat combine butter and marshmallows until melted, stirring often. Pour marshmallow mixture over popcorn mixture; stir until well coated. Form popcorn mixture into 12 balls; roll in "M&M's"® Chocolate Mini Baking Bits. Store in tightly covered container.

Makes 12 popcorn balls

Cranberry-Orange Snack Mix

Maple-Cinnamon Almonds

¼ **cup maple-flavored syrup**
3 **tablespoons butter**
2 **tablespoons sugar**
1½ **teaspoons ground cinnamon**
¼ **teaspoon salt**
1 **pound blanched whole almonds**
¼ **cup coarse decorating sugar* (optional)**

*Look for coarse sugar where either gourmet coffees or cake decorating supplies are sold.

1. Preheat oven to 325°F. Line two 15×10×1-inch jelly-roll pans with foil.

2. Combine syrup, butter, sugar, cinnamon and salt in heavy medium saucepan. Bring to a boil over high heat, stirring frequently. Boil 30 seconds. Remove from heat; stir in almonds with wooden spoon, tossing to coat evenly.

3. Spread almond mixture in single layer in one prepared pan. Bake about 40 minutes or until almonds are crisp and dry, stirring every 15 minutes. Immediately transfer almonds to remaining prepared pan; sprinkle evenly with coarse sugar. Cool completely. Store in airtight container at room temperature up to 1 week.

Makes about 3½ cups nuts

Note: If almonds become tacky upon storing, place on baking sheet lined with foil. Bake at 325°F 15 to 20 minutes; cool.

Oriental Snack Mix

4 **cups corn or rice cereal squares**
1 **cup honey roasted peanuts**
1 **can (5 ounces) chow mein noodles**
¼ **cup butter, melted**
3 **tablespoons teriyaki sauce**
1 **tablespoon dark sesame oil**
1 **teaspoon garlic powder**

1. Preheat oven to 250°F. Grease 13×9-inch baking pan; set aside.

2. Combine cereal, peanuts and noodles in medium bowl.

3. Whisk together butter, teriyaki sauce, oil and garlic powder in small bowl until well blended.

4. Drizzle butter mixture evenly over cereal mixture; stir until evenly coated.

5. Spread mixture in single layer in prepared baking pan. Bake 1 hour or until mix is lightly browned, stirring every 15 minutes. Cool completely in pan on wire rack. Store in airtight container at room temperature up to 2 weeks.

Makes 6 cups snack mix

Maple-Cinnamon Almonds

Harvest-Time Popcorn

2 tablespoons vegetable oil
1 cup popcorn kernels
2 cans (1¾ ounces each) shoestring
**   potatoes (3 cups)**
1 cup salted mixed nuts or peanuts
¼ cup margarine, melted
1 teaspoon dried dill weed
1 teaspoon Worcestershire sauce
½ teaspoon lemon-pepper seasoning
¼ teaspoon garlic powder
¼ teaspoon onion salt

1. Heat oil in 4-quart saucepan over high heat until hot. Add popcorn kernels. Cover pan; shake continuously over heat until popping stops. Popcorn should measure 2 quarts (8 cups). Do not add butter or salt.

2. Preheat oven to 325°F. Combine popcorn, shoestring potatoes and nuts in large roasting pan. Set aside.

3. Combine margarine, dill, Worcestershire, lemon-pepper seasoning, garlic powder and onion salt in small bowl. Pour evenly over popcorn mixture, stirring until evenly coated.

4. Bake 8 to 10 minutes, stirring once. Let stand at room temperature until cool. Store in airtight containers.   *Makes 12 cups popcorn mix*

Barbecued Peanuts

¼ cup barbecue sauce
2 tablespoons butter, melted
¾ teaspoon garlic salt
⅛ teaspoon ground red pepper*
1 jar (16 ounces) dry roasted lightly salted
**   peanuts**

*For spicy Barbecued Peanuts, increase ground red pepper to ¼ teaspoon.

1. Preheat oven to 325°F. Grease 13×9-inch baking pan; set aside.

2. Whisk barbecue sauce, melted butter, garlic salt and red pepper in medium bowl with wire whisk until well blended. Add peanuts; toss until evenly coated. Spread peanuts in single layer in prepared pan.

3. Bake 20 to 22 minutes or until peanuts are glazed, stirring occasionally. Cool completely in pan on wire rack, stirring occasionally to prevent peanuts from sticking together.

4. Spoon into clean, dry decorative tin; cover. Store tightly covered at room temperature up to 2 weeks.   *Makes about 4 cups peanuts*

Harvest-Time Popcorn

Candied Spiced Mixed Nuts

2 teaspoons CRISCO® Oil*
8 cups salted mixed nuts
1⅓ cups SMUCKER'S® Strawberry Jelly
4 tablespoons plus 2 teaspoons paprika, divided
6 teaspoons cumin, divided
1 cup brown sugar

Use your favorite Crisco Oil product.

1. Combine oil and nuts in medium bowl; set aside.

2. In small saucepan, melt SMUCKER'S® jelly over medium heat. Add 4 tablespoons paprika and 4 teaspoons cumin. Cook to hard ball stage, 260°F. measured on candy thermometer (or test for hard ball stage by dropping a teaspoon of mixture into glass of ice water; mixture will harden instantly if it has reached the proper temperature).

3. Immediately pour mixture over nuts. Stir with wooden spoon to evenly coat nut mixture. Cool for 5 minutes.

4. Combine brown sugar, remaining 2 teaspoons paprika and remaining 2 teaspoons cumin in small bowl. When cool enough to handle, sprinkle nuts with brown sugar mixture. Let cool completely.   *Makes 8 cups nuts*

Variation: Use SMUCKER'S® Orange Marmalade in place of the SMUCKER'S® Strawberry Jelly.

Party Mix with Cocoa

½ cup (1 stick) margarine
2 tablespoons sugar
2 tablespoons HERSHEY'S Cocoa
3 cups bite-size crisp wheat squares cereal
3 cups toasted oat cereal rings
2 cups miniature pretzels
1 cup salted peanuts
2 cups raisins

1. Place margarine in 4-quart microwave-safe bowl; microwave at HIGH (100%) 1 to 1½ minutes or until melted.

2. Stir in sugar and cocoa. Add cereals, pretzels and peanuts to margarine mixture; stir until well coated.

3. Microwave at HIGH 3 minutes, stirring every minute. Stir in raisins. Microwave at HIGH 3 minutes, stirring every minute. Cool completely. Store in airtight container at room temperature.   *Makes 10 cups mix*

Candied Spiced Mixed Nuts

Almond Butter Crunch Pop Corn

½ cup butter or margarine
 1 cup granulated sugar
¼ cup light corn syrup
¼ teaspoon salt
½ teaspoon vanilla
½ teaspoon butter extract
¼ teaspoon baking soda
2½ quarts popped JOLLY TIME® Pop Corn
1½ cups whole almonds, toasted*

To toast almonds, spread on large baking sheet and bake at 325°F 15 to 20 minutes.

Melt butter in medium saucepan. Stir in sugar, corn syrup and salt. Bring to a boil, stirring constantly. Boil 8 minutes over lowest heat possible to maintain a boil, stirring once. Remove from heat; stir in vanilla, butter extract and baking soda. Gradually pour over popped pop corn and nuts, mixing well. Turn into large shallow baking pan. Bake at 250°F 30 minutes, mixing well after 15 minutes. Allow to cool completely. Break apart and store in tightly covered container.

Makes about 3 quarts pop corn

Savory Nut Mix

⅓ CRISCO® Stick or ⅓ cup CRISCO® all-vegetable shortening
1½ teaspoons chili powder
 1 teaspoon Worcestershire sauce
½ teaspoon cayenne pepper
½ teaspoon garlic salt
½ teaspoon ground cinnamon
 2 cups cashews
 2 cups pecans

1. Heat oven to 300°F. In 11×7×1½-inch baking pan, melt shortening in oven. Stir in chili powder, Worcestershire sauce, cayenne, garlic salt and cinnamon.

2. Add cashews and pecans; toss to coat. Spread nuts evenly in pan.

3. Bake at 300°F for 20 to 25 minutes, stirring once or twice. Sprinkle nuts with additional salt, if desired.

4. Remove nuts to brown paper bag to cool. Shake occasionally while cooling. Store in airtight container for up to one week.

Makes 4 cups nuts

Variation: For a "hotter" nut add 4 or more drops cayenne pepper sauce to recipe.

Original Ranch® Oyster Crackers

1 box (16 ounces) oyster crackers
¼ cup vegetable oil
1 packet (1 ounce) HIDDEN VALLEY® The Original Ranch® Salad Dressing & Seasoning Mix

Place crackers in a gallon size Glad® Fresh Protection Bag. Pour oil over crackers and toss to coat. Add salad dressing mix; toss again until coated. Spread evenly on large baking sheet. Bake at 250°F for 15 to 20 minutes.

Makes 8 cups crackers

Helpful Hint

To quickly put the crunch back in your favorite snack food, simply place about 2½ cups of the snack food on a paper towel-lined microwavable dish. Heat at HIGH 20 to 40 seconds or just until warm. Let stand 5 minutes.

Butterscotch Party Mix

2 cups oven-toasted cereal squares
2 cups small pretzel twists
1 cup dry-roasted peanuts
1 cup (about 20) caramels, unwrapped, coarsely chopped
1 ⅔ cups (11-ounce package) NESTLÉ® TOLL HOUSE® Butterscotch Flavored Morsels

GREASE 13×9-inch baking pan with nonstick cooking spray.

COMBINE cereal, pretzels, peanuts and caramels in large bowl. Place morsels in medium, uncovered, microwave-safe bowl. Microwave on MEDIUM-HIGH (70%) power for 1 minute. STIR. The morsels may retain some of their original shape. If necessary, microwave at additional 10- to 15-second intervals, stirring just until smooth. Pour over cereal mixture; stir to coat evenly.

SPREAD mixture in prepared baking pan; let stand for 20 to 30 minutes or until firm. Break into small pieces.

Makes about 8 servings

Cheese Straws

½ cup (1 stick) butter, softened
⅛ teaspoon salt
   Dash ground red pepper
1 pound sharp Cheddar cheese, shredded,
      at room temperature
2 cups self-rising flour

Heat oven to 350°F. In mixer bowl, beat butter, salt and pepper until creamy. Add cheese; mix well. Gradually add flour, mixing until dough begins to form a ball. Form dough into ball with hands. Fit cookie press with small star plate; fill with dough according to manufacturer's directions. Press dough onto cookie sheets in 3-inch-long strips (or desired shapes). Bake 12 minutes or just until lightly browned. Cool completely on wire rack. Store tightly covered.

Makes about 10 dozen straws

Favorite recipe from **Southeast United Dairy Industry Association, Inc.**

Caramel Popcorn

3 quarts popped popcorn, unpopped
      kernels removed
1 cup packed light or dark brown sugar
½ cup FLEISCHMANN'S® Original
      Margarine
½ cup light corn syrup
½ teaspoon vanilla extract
½ teaspoon baking soda

1. Place popcorn in 14×10×2½-inch roasting pan; set aside.

2. Heat sugar, margarine and corn syrup in heavy 1½-quart saucepan over medium heat to a boil. Boil 5 minutes without stirring.

3. Remove from heat. Stir in vanilla and baking soda. Pour over popcorn; stir to coat evenly.

4. Bake in preheated 250°F oven for 1 hour, stirring every 15 minutes. Spread mixture onto baking sheet to cool, stirring occasionally to break apart. Store in airtight container.

Makes 3 quarts popcorn

Nutty Caramel Popcorn: Follow above recipe adding 2½ cups peanuts to popcorn.

Cheese Straws

Caramel Popcorn

Charming Cookies

A birthday, graduation or new job—whatever the occasion, cookies are the perfect treat to make it extra-special. From Apple Crisp Cookies to Dark Chocolate Dreams—these cookies are so delicious, they can turn any ordinary day into a celebration!

Banana Crescents

½ cup chopped almonds, toasted
6 tablespoons sugar, divided
½ cup margarine, cut into pieces
1½ cups plus 2 tablespoons all-purpose flour
⅛ teaspoon salt
1 extra-ripe, medium DOLE® Banana, peeled
2 to 3 ounces semisweet chocolate chips

• Pulverize almonds with 2 tablespoons sugar in blender.

• Beat margarine, almond mixture, remaining 4 tablespoons sugar, flour and salt until well blended.

• Purée banana in blender; add to almond mixture and mix until well blended.

• Shape tablespoonfuls of dough into logs, then shape into crescents. Place on ungreased cookie sheet. Bake at 375°F 25 minutes or until golden. Cool on wire rack.

• Melt chocolate in microwavable dish at MEDIUM (50% power) 1½ to 2 minutes, stirring once. Dip ends of cookies in chocolate. Refrigerate until chocolate is set.

Makes 2 dozen cookies

Banana Crescents

Ultimate Chippers

2½ **cups all-purpose flour**
1 **teaspoon baking soda**
½ **teaspoon salt**
1 **cup (2 sticks) butter, softened**
1 **cup packed light brown sugar**
½ **cup granulated sugar**
2 **eggs**
1 **tablespoon vanilla**
1 **cup semisweet chocolate chips**
1 **cup milk chocolate chips**
1 **cup white chocolate chips**
½ **cup coarsely chopped pecans (optional)**

1. Preheat oven to 375°F. Combine flour, baking soda and salt in medium bowl.

2. Beat butter, brown sugar and granulated sugar in large bowl until light and fluffy. Beat in eggs and vanilla. Add flour mixture to butter mixture; beat until well blended. Stir in chips and pecans, if desired.

3. Drop dough by heaping teaspoonfuls 2 inches apart onto ungreased cookie sheets. Bake 10 to 12 minutes or until edges are golden brown. Let cookies stand on cookie sheets 2 minutes. Remove cookies to wire racks; cool completely.

Makes about 6 dozen cookies

Cashew-Lemon Shortbread Cookies

½ **cup roasted cashews**
1 **cup (2 sticks) butter, softened**
½ **cup sugar**
2 **teaspoons lemon extract**
1 **teaspoon vanilla**
2 **cups all-purpose flour**
   Additional sugar

1. Preheat oven to 325°F. Place cashews in food processor; process until finely ground. Add butter, sugar, lemon extract and vanilla; process until well blended. Add flour; process using on/off pulses until dough is well blended and begins to form a ball.

2. Shape dough into 1½-inch balls; roll in additional sugar. Place about 2 inches apart on ungreased baking sheets; flatten.

3. Bake 17 to 19 minutes or just until set and edges are lightly browned. Remove cookies from baking sheets to wire racks; cool completely.

Makes 2 to 2½ dozen cookies

Ultimate Chippers

Ali's Oatmeal Cookies

1 Butter Flavor CRISCO® Stick or 1 cup
   Butter Flavor CRISCO® all-vegetable
   shortening
1 cup granulated sugar
1 cup firmly packed light brown sugar
2 eggs
1 teaspoon vanilla extract
1½ cups flour
1 teaspoon baking soda
¾ teaspoon salt
2½ cups uncooked oats (quick or old-
   fashioned)
1 cup finely chopped hazelnuts
1 cup finely diced dried apricots
1 cup chopped vanilla milk chips

1. Heat oven to 350°F.

2. Combine 1 cup shortening, granulated sugar, brown sugar, eggs and vanilla in large bowl. Beat at medium speed of electric mixer until well blended. Combine flour, baking soda and salt in small bowl; gradually add to creamed mixture at low speed. Beat until well blended.

3. Stir in oats, hazelnuts, apricots and vanilla milk chips with spoon; mix until just blended.

4. Shape dough into 1½-inch balls. Place 2 inches apart on ungreased baking sheet. Flatten balls slightly.

5. Bake 11 to 13 minutes or until just beginning to brown around edges and slightly moist in center. Cool on wire rack.
Makes about 4 dozen cookies

Thumbprint Cookies

1 cup butter or margarine
¼ cup sugar
1 teaspoon almond extract
2 cups all-purpose flour
½ teaspoon salt
1 cup finely chopped nuts (optional)
   SMUCKER'S® Preserves or Jams (any
   flavor)

1. Preheat oven to 400°F. Combine butter and sugar; beat until light and fluffy. Blend in almond extract. Add flour and salt; mix well.

2. Shape level tablespoonfuls of dough into balls; roll in nuts, if desired. Place on ungreased cookie sheets; flatten slightly. Indent centers; fill with preserves or jams.

3. Bake at 400°F for 10 to 12 minutes or just until lightly browned. *Makes 2½ dozen cookies*

Helpful Hint

For even baking and browning of cookies, it is best to place only one baking sheet at a time in the center of the oven. If you must bake more than one sheet at a time, rotate them from the top rack to the bottom rack halfway through the baking time.

Ali's Oatmeal Cookies

Spicy Ginger Molasses Cookies

    2 cups all-purpose flour
1½ teaspoons ground ginger
    1 teaspoon baking soda
    ½ teaspoon ground cloves
    ¼ teaspoon salt
    ¾ cup (1½ sticks) butter, softened
    1 cup sugar
    ¼ cup molasses
    1 egg
        Additional sugar
    ½ cup yogurt-covered raisins

1. Preheat oven to 375°F. Line cookie sheets with parchment paper.

2. Combine flour, ginger, baking soda, cloves and salt in small bowl; set aside.

3. Beat butter and 1 cup sugar in large bowl at medium speed of electric mixer until light and fluffy. Add molasses and egg; beat until well blended. Gradually beat in flour mixture at low speed just until blended.

4. Drop dough by level ¼ cupfuls about 3 inches apart onto prepared cookie sheets; flatten with bottom of glass dipped in additional sugar until about 2 inches in diameter. Press 8 to 9 yogurt-covered raisins into dough of each cookie.

5. Bake 11 to 12 minutes or until cookies are set. Cool 2 minutes on cookie sheets; slide parchment paper and cookies onto wire racks. Cool completely.

Makes about 1 dozen (4-inch) cookies

Butterscotch Sugar Drops

    1 cup (2 sticks) butter or margarine,
        softened
    1 cup sugar
    2 eggs
    ½ teaspoon vanilla extract
2½ cups all-purpose flour
    1 teaspoon baking soda
    ½ teaspoon salt
1¾ cups (11-ounce package) HERSHEY'S
        Butterscotch Chips
1¼ cups chopped dried apricots

1. Heat oven to 350°F.

2. Beat butter and sugar with electric mixer at medium speed in large bowl until well blended. Add eggs and vanilla; beat well. Stir together flour, baking soda and salt; gradually add to butter mixture, beating until well blended. Stir in chips and apricots. Drop by teaspoons onto ungreased cookie sheet.

3. Bake 8 to 10 minutes or until lightly browned around edges. Cool slightly. Remove to wire rack and cool completely.

Makes about 7 dozen cookies

Spicy Ginger Molasses Cookies

Cranberry Brown Sugar Cookies

- 2 cups firmly packed DOMINO® Dark Brown Sugar
- 1 cup butter or margarine, softened
- 2 eggs
- ½ cup sour cream
- 3½ cups all-purpose flour
- 1 teaspoon baking soda
- 1 teaspoon salt
- 1 teaspoon ground cinnamon
- ½ teaspoon ground nutmeg
- ¼ teaspoon ground cloves
- 1 cup dried cranberries (5 ounces)
- 1 cup golden raisins

Heat oven to 400°F. Lightly grease cookie sheets. Beat sugar and butter in large bowl until light and fluffy. Add eggs and sour cream; beat until creamy. Stir together flour, baking soda, salt, cinnamon, nutmeg and cloves in small bowl; gradually add to sugar mixture, beating until well mixed. Stir in cranberries and raisins. Drop by rounded teaspoonfuls onto cookie sheets. Bake 8 to 10 minutes or until lightly browned. Remove from cookie sheets to cooling racks. Cool completely.

Makes about 5 dozen cookies

Tip: If cranberries are exceptionally large, chop before adding to cookie dough.

Toffee Chunk Brownie Cookies

- 1 cup (2 sticks) butter
- 4 ounces unsweetened chocolate, coarsely chopped
- 1½ cups sugar
- 2 eggs
- 1 tablespoon vanilla
- 3 cups all-purpose flour
- ⅛ teaspoon salt
- 1½ cups coarsely chopped chocolate-covered toffee bars

1. Preheat oven to 350°F. Melt butter and chocolate in large saucepan over low heat, stirring until smooth. Remove from heat; cool slightly.

2. Stir sugar into chocolate mixture until smooth. Stir in eggs until well blended. Stir in vanilla until smooth. Stir in flour and salt just until blended. Fold in chopped toffee bars.

3. Drop heaping tablespoonfuls of dough 1½ inches apart onto ungreased cookie sheets.

4. Bake 12 minutes or until just set. Let cookies stand on cookie sheets 5 minutes; transfer to wire racks to cool completely. Store in airtight container.

Makes 36 cookies

Dark Chocolate Dreams

**16 ounces bittersweet chocolate candy bars
    or bittersweet chocolate chips**
¼ cup (½ stick) butter
½ cup all-purpose flour
¾ teaspoon ground cinnamon
½ teaspoon baking powder
¼ teaspoon salt
1½ cups sugar
3 eggs
1 teaspoon vanilla
**1 package (12 ounces) white chocolate
    chips**
1 cup chopped pecans, lightly toasted

1. Preheat oven to 350°F. Grease cookie sheets.

2. Coarsely chop chocolate bars; place in microwavable bowl. Add butter. Microwave at HIGH 2 minutes; stir. Microwave 1 to 2 minutes, stirring after 1 minute, or until chocolate is melted. Let cool slightly.

3. Combine flour, cinnamon, baking powder and salt in small bowl; set aside.

4. Beat sugar, eggs and vanilla at medium-high speed of electric mixer until very thick and mixture turns pale color, about 6 minutes.

5. Reduce speed to low; slowly beat in chocolate mixture until well blended. Gradually beat in flour mixture until blended. Fold in white chocolate chips and pecans.

6. Drop dough by level ⅓ cupfuls onto prepared cookie sheets, spacing 3 inches apart. Place piece of plastic wrap over dough; flatten dough with fingertips to form 4-inch circles. Remove plastic wrap.

7. Bake 12 minutes or until just firm to the touch and surface begins to crack. *Do not overbake.* Cool cookies 2 minutes on cookie sheets; transfer to wire racks. Cool completely.

Makes 10 to 12 (5-inch) cookies

Note: Cookies can be baked on ungreased cookie sheets lined with parchment paper. Cool cookies 2 minutes on cookie sheets; slide parchment paper and cookies onto countertop. Cool completely.

Helpful Hint

To toast the chopped pecans, spread them in a single layer on an ungreased baking sheet. Bake them in a preheated 350°F oven for 8 to 10 minutes or until they are golden brown, stirring frequently.

Apple Crisp Cookies

Cookies

  1 Butter Flavor CRISCO® Stick or 1 cup Butter Flavor CRISCO® all-vegetable shortening plus additional for greasing
  1 cup firmly packed light brown sugar
  1 teaspoon vanilla
  2½ cups oats (quick or old-fashioned, uncooked)
  2¼ cups all-purpose flour
  ½ teaspoon baking soda
  ½ teaspoon salt
  6 to 8 tablespoons water

Topping

  1 can (21 ounces) apple pie filling, finely chopped
  1 cup reserved crumb mixture
  ½ cup finely chopped pecans or walnuts

1. Heat oven to 375°F. Grease baking sheet with shortening. Place sheets of foil on countertop for cooling cookies.

2. For cookies, combine 1 cup shortening, brown sugar and vanilla in large bowl. Beat at medium speed of electric mixer until well blended.

3. Combine oats, flour, baking soda and salt. Add alternately with water to creamed mixture stirring with spoon. Mix well after each addition. (Mixture will be crumbly, but will hold together when shaped into small ball.) Add additional water if necessary. Reserve 1 cup dough for topping. Shape remaining dough into 1-inch balls. Place 2 inches apart on prepared baking sheet. Flatten to ⅛-inch thickness with floured bottom of glass. Smooth edges.

4. Bake at 375°F for 5 to 7 minutes or until light brown around edges and firm. *Do not overbake.* Remove from oven. Cool on baking sheet about 5 minutes.

5. For topping, place 1 measuring teaspoonful of pie filling in center of each cookie. Spread carefully to cover.

6. Combine 1 cup reserved crumbs and nuts in small bowl. Toss until mixed. Sprinkle over apple filling.

7. Return cookies to oven. Bake 5 minutes or until topping is light brown. *Do not overbake.* Cool 2 minutes on baking sheet. Remove cookies to foil to cool completely.

Makes about 3 dozen cookies

Apple Crisp Cookies

Chocolate Chips Thumbprint Cookies

1 cup HERSHEY'S Semi-Sweet Chocolate Chips, divided
½ cup sugar
¼ cup butter flavor shortening
¼ cup (½ stick) butter or margarine, softened
1 egg, separated
½ teaspoon vanilla extract
1 cup all-purpose flour
¼ teaspoon salt
1 cup finely chopped nuts

1. Heat oven to 350°F. Lightly grease cookie sheet. Place ¼ cup chocolate chips in small microwave-safe bowl. Microwave at HIGH (100%) 20 to 30 seconds or just until chocolate is melted and smooth when stirred; set aside to cool slightly.

2. Combine sugar, shortening, butter, reserved melted chocolate, egg yolk and vanilla; beat until well blended. Stir in flour and salt. Shape dough into 1-inch balls. With fork, lightly beat egg white. Dip each ball into egg white; roll in nuts to coat. Place about 1 inch apart on ungreased cookie sheet. Press center of each cookie with thumb to make indentation.

3. Bake 10 to 12 minutes or until set. Remove from oven; immediately place several chocolate chips in center of each cookie. Carefully remove from cookie sheet to wire rack. After several minutes, swirl melted chocolate in each thumbprint. Cool completely.

Makes about 2½ dozen cookies

Cherry Cashew Cookies

1 cup butter or margarine, softened
¾ cup granulated sugar
¾ cup packed brown sugar
2 eggs
1 teaspoon vanilla extract
2¼ cups all-purpose flour
1 teaspoon baking soda
1 (10-ounce) package vanilla milk chips (about 1⅔ cups)
1½ cups dried tart cherries
1 cup broken salted cashews

In large mixer bowl, combine butter, granulated sugar, brown sugar, eggs and vanilla. Mix with electric mixer on medium speed until well blended. Combine flour and baking soda; gradually add flour mixture to butter mixture. Stir in vanilla milk chips, dried cherries and cashews. Drop by rounded tablespoonfuls onto ungreased baking sheets.

Bake in preheated 375°F oven 12 to 15 minutes or until light golden brown. Cool on wire racks and store in airtight container.

Makes 4½ dozen cookies

Favorite recipe from **Cherry Marketing Institute**

Chocolate Chips Thumbprint Cookies

Brown-Eyed Susans

1 package (18 ounces) refrigerated sugar cookie dough
3 tablespoons unsweetened Dutch process cocoa powder
¼ cup all-purpose flour
1½ teaspoons banana extract
Yellow food coloring

1. Preheat oven to 350°F. Lightly grease cookie sheets. Remove dough from wrapper; reserve ⅔ of dough. Place remaining ⅓ dough in medium bowl; let stand at room temperature about 15 minutes.

2. For flower centers, add cocoa to dough in bowl; beat until well blended. Shape cocoa dough into 30 balls; place about 4 inches apart on prepared cookie sheets.

3. For flower petals, combine reserved dough, flour, banana extract and food coloring in medium bowl; beat until well blended and evenly colored. Divide dough into 30 pieces. Shape each piece into 6 ovals; place in circle around center ball on cookie sheet, leaving about ¼-inch space between petals and center ball. Pinch outside ends of yellow ovals to points for petal shapes. Repeat with remaining yellow pieces.

4. Bake 7 to 9 minutes or until firm but not browned. Cool completely on cookie sheets.

Makes 2½ dozen cookies

Note: "Dutch process" cocoa is unsweetened cocoa that has been treated with an alkali, giving it a darker appearance and a slightly less bitter flavor.

Powdered Sugar Cookies

1½ cups (3 sticks) I CAN'T BELIEVE IT'S NOT BUTTER!® Spread, softened
1⅓ cups confectioners' sugar
1 teaspoon vanilla extract
3½ cups all-purpose flour
1⅓ cups chopped walnuts
Additional confectioners' sugar

Preheat oven to 350°F.

In large bowl, with electric mixer, beat I Can't Believe It's Not Butter!® Spread and sugar until light and fluffy, about 5 minutes. Beat in vanilla, then flour, scraping sides occasionally, until blended. Stir in walnuts.

On *ungreased* baking sheets, drop dough by heaping teaspoonfuls, 2 inches apart. With palm of hand or spoon, gently flatten each cookie.

Bake 10 minutes or until light golden around edges. On wire rack, let stand 2 minutes; remove from sheets and cool completely. Sprinkle with additional sugar.

Makes 7 dozen cookies

Brown-Eyed Susans

Prized Peanut Butter Crunch Cookies

- 1 Butter Flavor CRISCO® Stick or 1 cup Butter Flavor CRISCO® all-vegetable shortening
- 2 cups firmly packed brown sugar
- 1 cup JIF® Extra Crunchy Peanut Butter
- 4 egg whites, lightly beaten
- 1 teaspoon vanilla
- 2 cups all-purpose flour
- 1 teaspoon baking soda
- ½ teaspoon baking powder
- 2 cups crisp rice cereal
- 1½ cups chopped peanuts
- 1 cup quick oats (not instant or old-fashioned)
- 1 cup flake coconut

1. Heat oven to .... foil on countert........

2. Com........ butter .... electric........ tes and van........

3. Comb........ powder. B........ speed un........ rice ....

4........ c........ sh........

5. Bak........ 8 to 10 mi........ bake. Remove cookies to foil to cool completely.

Makes about 4 dozen cookies

Oatmeal Toffee Cookies

- 1 cup (2 sticks) butter or margarine, softened
- 2 cups packed light brown sugar
- 2 eggs
- 2 teaspoons vanilla extract
- 1¾ cups all-purpose flour
- 1 teaspoon baking soda
- 1 teaspoon ground cinnamon
- ½ teaspoon salt
- 3 cups quick-cooking oats
- 1⅓ cups (8-ounce package) HEATH® BITS 'O BRICKLE Toffee Bits
- 1 cup MOUNDS® Sweetened Coconut Flakes (optional)

1. Heat oven to 375°F. Lightly grease cookie sheet. Beat butter, brown sugar, eggs and vanilla with electric mixer on medium speed in large bowl until well blended. Add flour, baking soda, cinnamon and salt; beat until blended.

2. Stir in oats, toffee bits and coconut, if desired, with spoon. Drop dough by rounded teaspoons about 2 inches apart onto prepared sheet.

3. Bake 8 to 10 minutes or until edges are lightly browned. Cool 1 minute. Remove to wire rack and cool completely.

Makes about 4 dozen cookies

Prized Peanut Butter Crunch Cookies

Original Nestlé® Toll House® Chocolate Chip Cookies

2¼ cups all-purpose flour
1 teaspoon baking soda
1 teaspoon salt
1 cup (2 sticks) butter or margarine, softened
¾ cup granulated sugar
¾ cup packed brown sugar
1 teaspoon vanilla extract
2 eggs
2 cups (12-ounce package) NESTLÉ® TOLL HOUSE® Semi-Sweet Chocolate Morsels
1 cup chopped nuts

PREHEAT oven to 375°F.

COMBINE flour, baking soda and salt in small bowl. Beat butter, granulated sugar, brown sugar and vanilla extract in large mixer bowl until creamy. Add eggs, one at a time, beating well after each addition. Gradually beat in flour mixture. Stir in morsels and nuts. Drop by rounded tablespoon onto ungreased baking sheets.

BAKE for 9 to 11 minutes or until golden brown. Cool on baking sheets for 2 minutes; remove to wire racks to cool completely.

Makes about 5 dozen cookies

Pan Cookie Variation: GREASE 15×10-inch jelly-roll pan. Prepare dough as above. Spread in prepared pan. Bake for 20 to 25 minutes or until golden brown. Cool in pan on wire rack. Makes 4 dozen bars.

Pineapple Oatmeal "Scotchies"

2 cans (8 ounces each) DOLE® Crushed Pineapple
1½ cups margarine, softened
1½ cups packed brown sugar
1 egg
3 cups rolled oats
2 cups all-purpose flour
1 teaspoon baking powder
1 teaspoon ground cinnamon
½ teaspoon salt
1 cup (6 ounces) butterscotch chips

• Drain crushed pineapple well; save juice for a beverage.

• Beat margarine and sugar until light and fluffy. Beat in egg and pineapple.

• Combine oats, flour, baking powder, cinnamon and salt; blend into pineapple mixture. Stir in chips.

• Drop by two tablespoonsful onto cookie sheets coated with cooking spray; flatten top with back of spoon. Bake at 375°F 20 minutes or until brown.

Makes 3½ dozen cookies

Original Nestlé® Toll House® Chocolate Chip Cookies

Nutty Oatmeal Raisin Chews

2 cups uncooked old-fashioned oats
1 cup all-purpose flour
1 cup packed brown sugar
1 cup light or dark raisins
1 cup walnut chips or finely chopped
  walnuts
½ cup canola oil
3 egg whites
1 teaspoon vanilla
¼ teaspoon salt

1. Preheat oven to 375°F. Lightly grease cookie sheets.

2. Place all ingredients in large bowl; beat until well blended. Using packed 1 tablespoon measuring spoon, drop dough 2 inches apart on prepared cookie sheets.

3. Dampen fingers with cold water and flatten dough into 2-inch rounds. Bake 12 to 14 minutes or until cookies are golden but not brown. Cool on cookie sheets 3 minutes. Transfer to wire racks to cool completely. Store in airtight container. *Makes 3½ to 4 dozen cookies*

Peanut Butter Kisses

1 cup granulated sugar
1 cup packed brown sugar
1 cup CRISCO® all-vegetable shortening
1 cup JIF® Peanut Butter
2 eggs
¼ cup milk
2 teaspoons vanilla
3½ cups sifted all-purpose flour
2 teaspoons baking soda
1 teaspoon salt
1 (11-ounce) package milk chocolate
  candies

1. Heat oven to 375°F.

2. Cream together granulated sugar, brown sugar, shortening and peanut butter. Add eggs, milk and vanilla; beat well.

3. Stir together flour, baking soda and salt; add to peanut butter mixture. Beat well.

4. Shape dough into 1-inch balls; roll in additional granulated sugar. Place on ungreased cookie sheet.

5. Bake at 375°F for 8 minutes. Remove from oven. Press one milk chocolate candy into center of each warm cookie.

6. Return to oven; bake 3 minutes longer.
Makes 6 to 7 dozen cookies

White Chocolate Chip Lemon Cookies

1 cup (2 sticks) margarine, softened
⅔ cup packed brown sugar
½ cup granulated sugar
1 egg
2 teaspoons lemon extract
2¼ cups all-purpose flour
¾ teaspoon baking soda
½ teaspoon salt
1 package (12 ounces) white chocolate
    chips

1. Preheat oven to 350°F. Line cookie sheets with parchment paper.

2. Beat margarine and sugars with electric mixer at medium speed until creamy. Add egg and lemon extract; beat until fluffy.

3. Combine flour, baking soda and salt in separate bowl. Gradually add to margarine mixture, beating until well blended. Stir in white chocolate chips.

4. Drop dough by tablespoonfuls onto prepared cookie sheets. Bake 8 to 10 minutes or until lightly browned. Cool on cookie sheets 2 minutes. Remove to wire racks; cool completely.   *Makes about 3 dozen cookies*

Macadamia Nut White Chip Pumpkin Cookies

2 cups all-purpose flour
2 teaspoons ground cinnamon
1 teaspoon ground cloves
1 teaspoon baking soda
1 cup (2 sticks) butter or margarine,
    softened
½ cup granulated sugar
½ cup packed brown sugar
1 cup LIBBY'S® 100% Pure Pumpkin
1 egg
2 teaspoons vanilla extract
2 cups (12-ounce package) NESTLÉ® TOLL
    HOUSE® Premier White Morsels
⅔ cup coarsely chopped macadamia nuts
    or walnuts, toasted

PREHEAT oven to 350°F.

COMBINE flour, cinnamon, cloves and baking soda in small bowl. Beat butter, granulated sugar and brown sugar in large mixer bowl until creamy. Beat in pumpkin, egg and vanilla extract until blended. Gradually beat in flour mixture. Stir in morsels and nuts. Drop by rounded tablespoon onto greased baking sheets; flatten slightly with back of spoon or greased bottom of glass dipped in granulated sugar.

BAKE for 11 to 14 minutes or until centers are set. Cool on baking sheets for 2 minutes; remove to wire racks to cool completely.
            Makes about 4 dozen cookies

Malted Milk Cookies

1 cup (2 sticks) butter, softened
¾ cup granulated sugar
¾ cup packed brown sugar
1 teaspoon baking soda
2 eggs
2 squares (1 ounce each) unsweetened chocolate, melted and cooled to room temperature
1 teaspoon vanilla
2¼ cups all-purpose flour
½ cup malted milk powder
1 cup chopped malted milk balls

1. Preheat oven to 375°F.

2. Beat butter 30 seconds with electric mixer at medium speed. Add granulated sugar, brown sugar and baking soda; beat until blended. Add eggs, chocolate and vanilla; beat until well blended.

3. Beat in as much flour as possible with mixer. Using spoon, stir in any remaining flour and malted milk powder. Stir in malted milk balls.

4. Drop dough by rounded teaspoonfuls 2½ inches apart onto ungreased cookie sheets. Bake about 10 minutes or until edges are firm. Cool on cookie sheets 1 minute. Remove to wire racks; cool completely.

Makes about 3 dozen cookies

Peanut Butter Chocolate Chippers

1 cup packed light brown sugar
1 cup creamy or chunky peanut butter
1 egg
¾ cup milk chocolate chips
Granulated sugar

1. Preheat oven to 350°F.

2. Combine brown sugar, peanut butter and egg in medium bowl; mix until well blended. Add chips; mix well.

3. Shape heaping tablespoonfuls of dough into 1½-inch balls. Place balls 2 inches apart on ungreased cookie sheets.

4. Dip table fork into granulated sugar; press criss-cross fashion onto each ball, flattening to ½-inch thickness.

5. Bake 12 minutes or until set. Let cookies stand on cookie sheets 2 minutes. Remove cookies with spatula to wire racks; cool completely.

Makes about 2 dozen cookies

Note: This simple recipe is unusual because it doesn't contain any flour—but it still makes great cookies!

Malted Milk Cookies

Peanut Butter Chocolate Chippers

Colorful Cookie Buttons

1½ cups (3 sticks) butter, softened
½ cup granulated sugar
½ cup firmly packed light brown sugar
2 egg yolks
1 teaspoon vanilla extract
3½ cups all-purpose flour
1½ teaspoons baking powder
½ teaspoon salt
1 cup "M&M's"® Chocolate Mini Baking Bits

Preheat oven to 350°F. In large bowl cream butter and sugars until light and fluffy; beat in egg yolks and vanilla. In medium bowl combine flour, baking powder and salt; add to creamed mixture. Shape dough into 72 balls. For each cookie, place one ball on ungreased cookie sheet and flatten. Place 8 to 10 "M&M's"® Chocolate Mini Baking Bits on dough. Flatten second ball and place over "M&M's"® Chocolate Mini Baking Bits, pressing top and bottom dough together. Decorate top with remaining "M&M's"® Chocolate Mini Baking Bits. Repeat with remaining dough balls and "M&M's"® Chocolate Mini Baking Bits, placing cookies about 2 inches apart on cookie sheet. Bake 17 to 18 minutes. Cool 2 minutes on cookie sheets; cool completely on wire racks. Store in tightly covered container.   *Makes 3 dozen cookies*

Drop Sugar Cookies

2½ cups sifted all-purpose flour
½ teaspoon ARM & HAMMER® Baking Soda
¼ teaspoon salt
½ cup butter, softened
¾ cup butter-flavored shortening
1 cup sugar
1 egg *or* ¼ cup egg substitute
1 teaspoon vanilla extract
2 teaspoons skim milk

Preheat oven to 400°F. Sift together flour, Baking Soda and salt; set aside. Beat butter and shortening in large bowl with electric mixer on medium speed until blended; gradually add sugar and continue beating until light and fluffy. Beat in egg and vanilla. Add flour mixture and beat until smooth; blend in milk. Drop dough by teaspoonfuls about 3 inches apart onto greased cookie sheets. Flatten with bottom of greased glass that has been dipped in sugar.

Bake 12 minutes or until edges are lightly browned. Cool on wire racks.

Makes about 5½ dozen cookies

Colorful Cookie Buttons

Hershey's Double Chocolate Mini Kisses® Cookies

1 cup (2 sticks) butter or margarine, softened
1½ cups sugar
2 eggs
2 teaspoons vanilla extract
2 cups all-purpose flour
⅔ cup HERSHEY'S Cocoa
¾ teaspoon baking soda
¼ teaspoon salt
1¾ cups (10-ounce package) HERSHEY'S MINI KISSES® Milk Chocolates
½ cup coarsely chopped nuts (optional)

1. Heat oven to 350°F.

2. Beat butter, sugar, eggs and vanilla with electric mixer on medium speed in large bowl until light and fluffy. Stir together flour, cocoa, baking soda and salt; add to butter mixture, beating until well blended. Stir in chocolates and nuts, if desired. Drop by tablespoonfuls onto ungreased cookie sheet.

3. Bake 8 to 10 minutes or just until set. Cool slightly. Remove to wire rack and cool completely.   *Makes about 3½ dozen cookies*

Chocolate-Orange Chip Cookies

1¼ cups packed brown sugar
½ Butter Flavor CRISCO® Stick or ½ cup Butter Flavor CRISCO® all-vegetable shortening
2 squares (1 ounce each) unsweetened chocolate, melted and cooled
1 egg
2 tablespoons orange juice concentrate
1 teaspoon grated orange peel
1 teaspoon vanilla
1½ cups all-purpose flour
¾ teaspoon baking soda
¼ teaspoon salt
1 cup semisweet chocolate chips
½ cup blanched slivered almonds

1. Heat oven to 375°F. Place sheets of foil on countertop for cooling cookies.

2. Combine brown sugar, ½ cup shortening and melted chocolate in large bowl. Beat at medium speed of electric mixer until well blended. Beat in egg, orange juice concentrate, orange peel and vanilla.

3. Combine flour, baking soda and salt. Beat into shortening mixture at low speed until well blended. Stir in chocolate chips and nuts.

4. Drop tablespoonfuls of dough 2 inches apart onto ungreased baking sheets.

5. Bake one baking sheet at a time at 375°F for 7 to 9 minutes or until set. *Do not overbake.* Cool 2 minutes on baking sheets. Remove cookies to foil to cool completely.
     Makes about 3½ dozen cookies

Hershey's Double Chocolate Mini Kisses® Cookies

Double Chocolate Walnut Drops

¾ cup (1½ sticks) butter or margarine, softened
¾ cup granulated sugar
¾ cup firmly packed light brown sugar
1 egg
1 teaspoon vanilla extract
2¼ cups all-purpose flour
⅓ cup unsweetened cocoa powder
1 teaspoon baking soda
½ teaspoon salt
1¾ cups "M&M's"® Chocolate Mini Baking Bits
1 cup coarsely chopped English or black walnuts

Preheat oven to 350°F. Lightly grease cookie sheets; set aside. In large bowl cream butter and sugars until light and fluffy; beat in egg and vanilla. In medium bowl combine flour, cocoa powder, baking soda and salt; add to creamed mixture. Stir in "M&M's"® Chocolate Mini Baking Bits and nuts. Drop by heaping tablespoonfuls about 2 inches apart onto prepared cookie sheets. Bake 12 to 14 minutes for chewy cookies or 14 to 16 minutes for crispy cookies. Cool completely on wire racks. Store in tightly covered container.

Makes about 4 dozen cookies

Variation: Shape dough into 2-inch-thick roll. Cover with plastic wrap; refrigerate. When ready to bake, slice dough into ¼-inch-thick slices and bake as directed.

Coconut Macaroons

1 (14-ounce) can EAGLE BRAND®
   Sweetened Condensed Milk
   (NOT evaporated milk)
1 egg white
2 teaspoons vanilla extract
1 to 1½ teaspoons almond extract
2 (7-ounce) packages flaked coconut
   (5⅓ cups)

1. Preheat oven to 325°F. Line baking sheets with foil; grease and flour foil. Set aside.

2. In large mixing bowl, combine EAGLE BRAND®, egg white, vanilla and almond extract. Stir in coconut. Drop by rounded teaspoonfuls onto prepared sheets; with spoon, slightly flatten each mound.

3. Bake 15 to 17 minutes or until golden. Remove from baking sheets; cool on wire racks. Store loosely covered at room temperature.

Makes about 4 dozen cookies

Double Chocolate Walnut Drops

Chunky Chocolate Chip Peanut Butter Cookies

1¼ cups all-purpose flour
½ teaspoon baking soda
½ teaspoon ground cinnamon
½ teaspoon salt
¾ cup (1½ sticks) butter or margarine, softened
½ cup packed brown sugar
½ cup granulated sugar
½ cup creamy peanut butter
1 egg
1 teaspoon vanilla extract
2 cups (12-ounce package) NESTLÉ® TOLL HOUSE® Semi-Sweet Chocolate Morsels
½ cup coarsely chopped peanuts

PREHEAT oven to 375°F.

COMBINE flour, baking soda, cinnamon and salt in small bowl. Beat butter, brown sugar, granulated sugar and peanut butter in large mixer bowl until creamy. Beat in egg and vanilla extract. Gradually beat in flour mixture. Stir in morsels and peanuts.

DROP dough by rounded tablespoon onto ungreased baking sheets. Press down slightly to flatten into 2-inch circles.

BAKE for 7 to 10 minutes or until edges are set but centers are still soft. Cool on baking sheets for 4 minutes; remove to wire racks to cool completely.   *Makes about 3 dozen cookies*

Oatmeal Candied Chippers

¾ cup (1½ sticks) butter, softened
¾ cup granulated sugar
¾ cup packed light brown sugar
3 tablespoons milk
1 egg
2 teaspoons vanilla
¾ cup all-purpose flour
¾ teaspoon salt
½ teaspoon baking soda
3 cups uncooked old-fashioned or quick oats
1⅓ cups (10-ounce package) candy-coated semisweet chocolate chips or candy-coated chocolate pieces

1. Preheat oven to 375°F. Grease cookie sheets; set aside. Beat butter, granulated sugar and brown sugar in large bowl until light and fluffy. Add milk, egg and vanilla; beat well. Add flour, salt and baking soda. Beat until well blended. Stir in oats and chocolate chips.

2. Drop by rounded tablespoonfuls 2 inches apart onto prepared cookie sheets. Bake 10 to 12 minutes or until edges are golden brown. Let cookies stand 2 minutes on cookie sheets. Remove to wire racks; cool completely.
Makes about 4 dozen cookies

Chunky Chocolate Chip Peanut Butter Cookies

Dreamy Chocolate Chip Cookies

1¼ cups firmly packed brown sugar
¾ Butter Flavor CRISCO® Stick or ¾ cup Butter Flavor CRISCO® all-vegetable shortening
3 eggs, lightly beaten
2 teaspoons vanilla
1 (4-ounce) package German sweet chocolate, melted, cooled
3 cups all-purpose flour
1 teaspoon baking soda
½ teaspoon salt
1 (11½-ounce) package milk chocolate chips
1 (10-ounce) package premium semisweet chocolate chips
1 cup coarsely chopped macadamia nuts

1. Heat oven to 375°F. Place sheets of foil on countertop for cooling cookies.

2. Combine brown sugar, ¾ cup shortening, eggs and vanilla in large bowl. Beat at low speed of electric mixer until blended. Increase speed to high. Beat 2 minutes. Add melted chocolate. Mix until well blended.

3. Combine flour, baking soda and salt. Add gradually to shortening mixture at low speed.

4. Stir in chocolate chips and nuts with spoon. Drop by rounded tablespoonfuls 3 inches apart onto ungreased baking sheets.

5. Bake at 375°F for 9 to 11 minutes or until set. *Do not overbake.* Cool 2 minutes on baking sheets. Remove cookies to foil to cool completely. *Makes about 3 dozen cookies*

Hershey's Double Chocolate Mint Cookies

⅔ cup butter or margarine, softened
1 cup sugar
1 egg
1 teaspoon vanilla extract
1 cup all-purpose flour
½ cup HERSHEY'S Cocoa
½ teaspoon baking soda
¼ teaspoon salt
1⅔ cups (10-ounce package) HERSHEY'S Mint Chocolate Chips

1. Heat oven to 350°F.

2. Beat butter and sugar with electric mixer on medium speed in large bowl until creamy. Add egg and vanilla; beat well. Stir together flour, cocoa, baking soda and salt; gradually add to butter mixture, beating until well blended. Stir in mint chocolate chips. Drop by rounded teaspoons onto ungreased cookie sheet.

3. Bake 8 to 9 minutes or just until set; do not overbake. Cool slightly. Remove to wire rack and cool completely. *Makes about 2½ dozen cookies*

Dreamy Chocolate Chip Cookies

Blissful Brownies & Bars

What can you give the person who has everything? Indulge them with a beautiful box filled with decadent brownies or melt-in-your-mouth bars. It's a gift they'll ask for again and again!

White Chocolate Squares

- 1 (12-ounce) package white chocolate chips, divided
- ¼ cup (½ stick) butter or margarine
- 1 (14-ounce) can EAGLE BRAND® Sweetened Condensed Milk (NOT evaporated milk)
- 1 egg
- 1 teaspoon vanilla extract
- 2 cups all-purpose flour
- ½ teaspoon baking powder
- 1 cup chopped pecans, toasted
- Powdered sugar

1. Preheat oven to 350°F. Grease 13×9-inch baking pan. In large saucepan over low heat, melt 1 cup chips and butter. Stir in EAGLE BRAND®, egg and vanilla. Stir in flour and baking powder until blended. Stir in pecans and remaining chips. Spoon mixture into prepared pan.

2. Bake 20 to 25 minutes. Cool. Sprinkle with powdered sugar; cut into squares. Store covered at room temperature. *Makes 2 dozen squares*

White Chocolate Squares

Almond Brownies

½ cup (1 stick) butter
2 squares (1 ounce each) unsweetened baking chocolate
2 eggs
1 cup firmly packed light brown sugar
¼ teaspoon almond extract
½ cup all-purpose flour
1½ cups "M&M's"® Chocolate Mini Baking Bits, divided
½ cup slivered almonds, toasted and divided
Chocolate Glaze (recipe follows)

Preheat oven to 350°F. Grease and flour 8×8×2-inch baking pan; set aside. In small saucepan melt butter and chocolate over low heat; stir to blend. Remove from heat; let cool. In medium bowl beat eggs and brown sugar until well blended; stir in chocolate mixture and almond extract. Add flour. Stir in 1 cup "M&M's"® Chocolate Mini Baking Bits and ¼ cup almonds. Spread batter evenly in prepared pan. Bake 25 to 28 minutes or until firm in center. Cool completely on wire rack. Prepare Chocolate Glaze. Spread over brownies; decorate with remaining ½ cup "M&M's"® Chocolate Mini Baking Bits and remaining ¼ cup almonds. Cut into bars. Store in tightly covered container. *Makes 16 brownies*

Chocolate Glaze: In small saucepan over low heat combine 4 teaspoons water and 1 tablespoon butter until it comes to a boil. Stir in 4 teaspoons unsweetened cocoa powder. Gradually stir in ½ cup powdered sugar until smooth. Remove from heat; stir in ¼ teaspoon vanilla extract. Let glaze cool slightly.

Walnut Apple Dumpling Bars

6 tablespoons (¾ stick) butter or margarine
1 cup packed light brown sugar
1 cup all-purpose flour
1 teaspoon baking powder
1½ teaspoons ground cinnamon
2 eggs
1½ cups coarsely chopped California walnuts
1 Granny Smith or pippin apple, coarsely grated* (about 1 cup lightly packed)
Powdered sugar

It's not necessary to peel or core apple. Use hand-held grater, turning apple as you go, until only core remains.

Preheat oven to 350°F.

Melt butter in 3-quart saucepan. Add sugar. Stir until sugar is melted and mixture begins to bubble; cool. In small bowl combine flour, baking powder and cinnamon; mix to blend thoroughly. Beat eggs into butter mixture in saucepan, 1 at a time, then add flour mixture. Add walnuts and apple. Turn into buttered and floured 9-inch square baking pan; smooth top. Bake 25 to 35 minutes until pick inserted in center comes out clean and edges begin to pull away from sides of pan. Cool completely on rack. Cut into 3×1-inch bars. Garnish with powdered sugar. *Makes 24 bars*

Favorite recipe from **Walnut Marketing Board**

Almond Brownies

Razz-Ma-Tazz Bars

½ cup (1 stick) butter or margarine
2 cups (12-ounce package) NESTLÉ® TOLL
   HOUSE® Premier White Morsels,
   divided
2 eggs
½ cup granulated sugar
1 cup all-purpose flour
½ teaspoon salt
½ teaspoon almond extract
½ cup seedless raspberry jam
¼ cup toasted sliced almonds

PREHEAT oven to 325°F. Grease and sugar 9-inch square baking pan.

MELT butter in medium, microwave-safe bowl on HIGH (100%) power for 1 minute; stir. Add *1 cup* morsels; let stand. Do not stir.

BEAT eggs in large mixer bowl until foamy. Add sugar; beat until light lemon colored, about 5 minutes. Stir in morsel-butter mixture. Add flour, salt and almond extract; mix at low speed until combined. Spread ⅔ of batter into prepared pan.

BAKE for 15 to 17 minutes or until light golden brown around edges. Remove from oven to wire rack.

HEAT jam in small, microwave-safe bowl on HIGH (100%) power for 30 seconds; stir. Spread jam over warm crust. Stir *remaining* morsels into *remaining* batter. Drop spoonfuls of batter over jam. Sprinkle with almonds.

BAKE for 25 to 30 minutes or until edges are browned. Cool completely in pan on wire rack. Cut into bars.   *Makes 16 bars*

Mocha Fudge Brownies

3 squares (1 ounce each) semisweet
   chocolate
¾ cup sugar
½ cup (1 stick) butter, softened
2 eggs
2 teaspoons instant espresso coffee
   powder
1 teaspoon vanilla
½ cup all-purpose flour
½ cup chopped toasted almonds
1 cup (6 ounces) milk chocolate chips,
   divided

1. Preheat oven to 350°F. Grease 8-inch square baking pan.

2. Melt semisweet chocolate in top of double boiler over hot, not boiling, water. Remove from heat; let cool slightly.

3. Beat sugar and butter in medium bowl until well blended. Add eggs; beat until light and fluffy. Add melted chocolate, coffee powder and vanilla; beat until well blended. Stir in flour, almonds and ½ cup chocolate chips. Spread batter evenly in prepared pan.

4. Bake 25 minutes or just until firm in center. Remove from oven; sprinkle with remaining ½ cup chocolate chips. Let stand until chips melt; spread chips evenly over brownies. Cool completely in pan on wire rack. Cut into 2-inch squares.   *Makes 16 brownies*

Razz-Ma-Tazz Bars

Almond Chinese Chews

1 cup granulated sugar
3 eggs, lightly beaten
1 can SOLO® or 1 jar BAKER® Almond Filling
¾ cup all-purpose flour
1 teaspoon baking powder
¼ teaspoon salt
Powdered sugar

1. Preheat oven to 300°F. Grease 13×9-inch baking pan; set aside.

2. Beat granulated sugar and eggs in medium-size bowl with electric mixer until thoroughly blended. Add almond filling; beat until blended. Sift together flour, baking powder and salt; fold into almond mixture. Spread batter evenly in prepared pan.

3. Bake 40 to 45 minutes or until wooden toothpick inserted in center comes out clean. Cool completely in pan on wire rack. Cut into 2×1½-inch bars; dust with powdered sugar.

Makes about 3 dozen bars

Magic Apple Cookie Bars

¼ Butter Flavor CRISCO® Stick or ¼ cup Butter Flavor CRISCO® all-vegetable shortening plus additional for greasing
1 cup quick oats (not instant or old-fashioned), uncooked
¾ cup graham cracker crumbs
1½ cups very finely chopped peeled Granny Smith or other firm, tart cooking apples
½ cup butterscotch chips (optional)
½ cup flake coconut
½ cup finely chopped nuts
1 can (14 ounces) sweetened condensed milk (not evaporated milk)

1. Heat oven to 350°F. Grease 11×7×2-inch glass baking dish with shortening. Place wire rack on countertop for cooling bars.

2. Combine oats, graham cracker crumbs and ¼ cup shortening. Stir well. Press firmly on bottom of prepared dish. Top with apples, butterscotch chips, if desired, coconut and nuts. Pour condensed milk over top.

3. Bake at 350°F for 30 to 35 minutes or until lightly browned. *Do not overbake.* Loosen from sides of dish while still warm. Cool completely in dish on wire rack. Cut into 2×1½-inch bars. Serve immediately or refrigerate.

Makes 3 dozen bars

Almond Chinese Chews

Layers of Love Chocolate Brownies

¾ **cup all-purpose flour**
¾ **cup NESTLÉ® TOLL HOUSE® Baking Cocoa**
¼ **teaspoon salt**
½ **cup (1 stick) butter, cut in pieces**
½ **cup granulated sugar**
½ **cup packed brown sugar**
3 **eggs,** *divided*
2 **teaspoons vanilla extract**
1 **cup chopped pecans**
¾ **cup NESTLÉ® TOLL HOUSE® Premier White Morsels**
½ **cup caramel ice cream topping**
¾ **cup NESTLÉ® TOLL HOUSE® Semi-Sweet Chocolate Morsels**

PREHEAT oven to 350°F. Grease 8-inch square baking pan.

COMBINE flour, cocoa and salt in small bowl. Beat butter, granulated sugar and brown sugar in large mixer bowl until creamy. Add *2 eggs,* one at a time, beating well after each addition. Add vanilla extract; mix well. Gradually beat in flour mixture. Reserve *¾ cup* batter. Spread *remaining* batter into prepared baking pan. Sprinkle pecans and white morsels over batter. Drizzle caramel topping over top. Beat *remaining* egg and *reserved* batter in same large bowl until light in color. Stir in semi-sweet morsels. Spread evenly over caramel topping.

BAKE for 30 to 35 minutes or until center is set. Cool completely in pan on wire rack. Cut into squares. *Makes 16 brownies*

Tropical Coconut Squares

1 **cup butter, softened**
½ **cup granulated sugar**
2 **egg yolks**
¼ **teaspoon salt**
2¼ **cups plus 3 tablespoons all-purpose flour, divided**
½ **teaspoon baking powder**
1½ **cups packed light brown sugar**
3 **eggs**
1 **teaspoon vanilla**
1½ **cups macadamia nuts**
2 **cups flaked coconut**

1. Preheat oven to 350°F. Grease 15×10-inch jelly-roll pan.

2. Beat butter and granulated sugar in large bowl until light and fluffy. Beat in egg yolks and salt. Gradually add 2¼ cups flour; beat until well blended. Spread dough in prepared pan. Bake 16 to 18 minutes or until golden brown.

3. Combine remaining 3 tablespoons flour and baking powder in small bowl. Beat brown sugar and whole eggs in large bowl until very thick. Beat in vanilla. Gradually add flour mixture; beat until well blended. Stir in nuts.

4. Spread batter evenly over hot crust; sprinkle with coconut. Bake 20 to 22 minutes or until top is golden brown and puffed.

5. Remove pan to wire rack to cool completely. Cut into 2-inch squares. Store squares tightly covered at room temperature or freeze up to 3 months. *Makes about 40 squares*

Layers of Love Chocolate Brownies

Dulce de Leche Blondies

2 cups all-purpose flour
1 teaspoon baking soda
1 teaspoon salt
1 cup (2 sticks) unsalted butter, softened
1 cup firmly packed brown sugar
2 eggs
1½ teaspoons vanilla
1 (14-ounce) package caramels
½ cup evaporated milk

1. Preheat oven to 350°F. Grease 13×9-inch baking pan. Sift together flour, baking soda and salt in medium bowl; set aside.

2. Beat butter and sugar in large bowl until creamy. Add eggs and vanilla; beat until smooth. Gradually stir in flour mixture. Spread ½ to ⅔ of batter in prepared pan. Bake 7 to 8 minutes. Let cool 5 minutes on wire rack.

3. Meanwhile, melt caramels with evaporated milk in nonstick saucepan over very low heat. Reserve 2 tablespoons. Pour remaining caramel mixture over baked bottom layer. Drop dollops of remaining batter over caramel layer; swirl slightly with knife.

4. Bake 25 minutes or until golden brown. Cool in pan on wire rack. When completely cooled, cut into squares. Reheat reserved caramel, if necessary; drizzle over blondies.

Makes about 3 dozen blondies

Fudgy Cheesecake Swirl Brownies

¾ cup (1½ sticks) butter or margarine
2 bars (2 ounces *each*) NESTLÉ® TOLL HOUSE® Unsweetened Chocolate Baking Bars, broken into pieces
2¼ cups granulated sugar, *divided*
4 eggs, *divided*
1¾ cups all-purpose flour
1 package (8 ounces) cream cheese, softened
1 teaspoon vanilla extract

PREHEAT oven to 350°F. Grease 13×9-inch baking pan.

MELT butter and baking bars in medium, *heavy-duty* saucepan over low heat, stirring until smooth. Cool to room temperature. Stir in 1¾ cups sugar. Beat in 3 eggs; stir in flour. Spread into prepared baking pan.

BEAT cream cheese and *remaining ½ cup* sugar in small mixer bowl. Beat in *remaining* egg and vanilla extract. Pour over chocolate mixture; deeply swirl batters with knife.

BAKE for 30 to 35 minutes or until wooden pick inserted near center comes out slightly sticky. Cool completely in pan on wire rack.

Makes 2 dozen brownies

Dulce de Leche Blondies

Banana Split Bars

2 extra-ripe, medium DOLE® Bananas, peeled
2 cups all-purpose flour
1 cup granulated sugar
¾ teaspoon baking soda
½ teaspoon salt
½ teaspoon ground cinnamon
1 can (8 ounces) DOLE® Crushed Pineapple, undrained
2 eggs
½ cup vegetable oil
1 teaspoon vanilla extract
¼ cup maraschino cherries, drained, halved
Creamy Vanilla Frosting (recipe follows)

Preheat oven to 350°F. In food processor or blender container, process bananas until puréed (1 cup). In large bowl, combine flour, granulated sugar, baking soda, salt and cinnamon. Add puréed bananas, undrained crushed pineapple, eggs, oil and vanilla. Mix until well blended. Stir in cherries. Pour into greased and floured 13×9-inch baking pan. Bake 30 to 35 minutes. Cool in pan on wire rack 30 minutes. Spread with Creamy Vanilla Frosting. Cut into bars.

Makes about 36 bars

Creamy Vanilla Frosting

¼ cup margarine
3 to 4 tablespoons milk
3 cups powdered sugar
1 teaspoon vanilla extract

In small saucepan, heat margarine and milk until margarine melts. Remove from heat. Stir in powdered sugar and vanilla. Beat until smooth.

Sensational Peppermint Pattie Brownies

24 small (1½-inch) YORK® Peppermint Patties
1½ cups (3 sticks) butter or margarine, melted
3 cups sugar
1 tablespoon vanilla extract
5 eggs
2 cups all-purpose flour
1 cup HERSHEY'S Cocoa
1 teaspoon baking powder
1 teaspoon salt

1. Heat oven to 350°F. Remove wrappers from peppermint patties. Grease 13×9×2-inch baking pan.

2. Stir together butter, sugar and vanilla in large bowl. Add eggs; beat until well blended. Stir together flour, cocoa, baking powder and salt; gradually add to butter mixture, blending well. Reserve 2 cups batter. Spread remaining batter into prepared pan. Arrange peppermint patties about ½ inch apart in single layer over batter. Spread reserved batter over patties.

3. Bake 50 to 55 minutes or until brownies pull away from sides of pan. Cool completely in pan on wire rack. *Makes about 36 brownies*

Chewy Macadamia Nut Blondies

¾ **Butter Flavor CRISCO® Stick or ¾ cup Butter Flavor CRISCO® all-vegetable shortening**
1 cup firmly packed light brown sugar
1 egg
1 teaspoon vanilla
1 teaspoon almond extract
1 cup all-purpose flour
½ teaspoon baking soda
⅛ teaspoon salt
6 ounces white chocolate chips
1 cup chopped macadamia nuts

1. Heat oven to 325°F. Place wire rack on countertop for cooling bars.

2. Combine ¾ cup shortening and sugar in large bowl. Beat at medium speed of electric mixer until well blended. Beat in egg, vanilla and almond extract until well blended.

3. Combine flour, baking soda and salt in small bowl. Add to creamed mixture until just incorporated. *Do not overmix.* Fold in white chocolate chips and nuts until just blended.

4. Spray 9-inch square baking pan with CRISCO® No-Stick Cooking Spray. Pour batter into prepared pan. Bake at 325°F for 25 to 30 minutes or until toothpick inserted in center comes out almost dry and top is golden. *Do not overbake or overbrown.*

5. Cool completely in pan on wire rack. Cut into bars.
Makes about 16 bars

Maraschino Brownies

1 (21½- to 23½-ounce) package brownie mix (13×9 pan size), plus ingredients to prepare mix
1 (8-ounce) container plain low-fat yogurt
1 (10-ounce) jar maraschino cherries, drained

Prepare brownie mix according to package directions, adding yogurt with liquid ingredients; mix well. Stir in cherries. Spoon batter into greased and floured 13×9×2-inch baking pan. Make sure cherries are evenly distributed.

Bake in preheated 350°F oven 28 to 30 minutes. *Do not overbake.* Brownies will be moist and cannot be tested with wooden pick.
Makes 2 dozen bars

Favorite recipe from **Cherry Marketing Institute**

Helpful Hint

For easy removal of brownies and bar cookies (and no cleanup!), line the baking pan with foil and leave at least 3 inches hanging over each end. Use the foil to lift out the treats, place them on a cutting board and carefully remove the foil. Then simply cut them into pieces.

Peanutty Cranberry Bars

½ cup (1 stick) butter or margarine,
   softened
½ cup granulated sugar
¼ cup packed light brown sugar
1 cup all-purpose flour
1 cup quick-cooking rolled oats
¼ teaspoon baking soda
¼ teaspoon salt
1 cup REESE'S® Peanut Butter Chips
1½ cups fresh or frozen whole cranberries
⅔ cup light corn syrup
½ cup water
1 teaspoon vanilla extract

1. Heat oven to 350°F. Grease 8-inch square baking pan.

2. Beat butter, granulated sugar and brown sugar in medium bowl until fluffy. Stir together flour, oats, baking soda and salt; gradually add to butter mixture, mixing until mixture is consistency of coarse crumbs. Stir in peanut butter chips.

3. Reserve 1½ cups mixture for crumb topping. Firmly press remaining mixture evenly into prepared pan. Bake 15 minutes or until set.

4. Meanwhile, in medium saucepan, combine cranberries, corn syrup and water. Cook over medium heat, stirring occasionally, until mixture boils. Reduce heat; simmer 15 minutes, stirring occasionally. Remove from heat. Stir in vanilla. Spread evenly over baked layer. Sprinkle reserved crumb topping evenly over top.

5. Return to oven. Bake 15 to 20 minutes or until set. Cool completely in pan on wire rack. Cut into bars.   *Makes about 16 bars*

Orange Chess Bars

Crust
1 package DUNCAN HINES® Moist Deluxe®
   Orange Supreme Cake Mix
½ cup vegetable oil
⅓ cup chopped pecans
Topping
1 pound (3½ to 4 cups) confectioners'
   sugar
1 package (8 ounces) cream cheese,
   softened
2 eggs
2 teaspoons grated orange peel

1. Preheat oven to 350°F. Grease 13×9-inch baking pan.

2. For crust, combine cake mix, oil and pecans in large bowl. Stir until blended. (Mixture will be crumbly.) Press on bottom of prepared pan.

3. For topping, combine confectioners' sugar and cream cheese in large bowl. Beat at low speed with electric mixer until blended. Add eggs and orange peel. Beat at low speed until blended. Pour over crust. Bake 30 to 35 minutes or until topping is set. Cool. Refrigerate until ready to serve. Cut into bars.

Makes about 24 bars

Peanutty Cranberry Bars

Toffee-Top Cheesecake Bars

1¼ cups all-purpose flour
1 cup powdered sugar
½ cup unsweetened cocoa
¼ teaspoon baking soda
¾ cup (1½ sticks) butter or margarine
1 (8-ounce) package cream cheese, softened
1 (14-ounce) can EAGLE BRAND® Sweetened Condensed Milk (NOT evaporated milk)
2 eggs
1 teaspoon vanilla extract
1½ cups (8-ounce package) English toffee bits, divided

1. Preheat oven to 350°F. In medium mixing bowl, combine flour, powdered sugar, cocoa and baking soda; cut in butter until mixture is crumbly. Press firmly on bottom of ungreased 13×9-inch baking pan. Bake 15 minutes.

2. In large mixing bowl, beat cream cheese until fluffy. Add EAGLE BRAND®, eggs and vanilla; beat until smooth. Stir in 1 cup English toffee bits. Pour mixture over hot crust. Bake 25 minutes or until set and edges just begin to brown.

3. Cool 15 minutes. Sprinkle remaining ½ cup English toffee bits evenly over top. Cool completely. Refrigerate several hours or until cold. Store leftovers covered in refrigerator.

Makes about 3 dozen bars

Reese's® Peanut Butter and Milk Chocolate Chip Blondies

1½ cups packed light brown sugar
1 cup (2 sticks) butter or margarine, melted
½ cup granulated sugar
2 eggs
2 teaspoons vanilla extract
2 cups all-purpose flour
1 teaspoon salt
1¾ cups (11-ounce package) REESE'S® Peanut Butter and Milk Chocolate Chips, divided
¼ teaspoon shortening (do not use butter, margarine, spread or oil)

1. Heat oven to 350°F. Grease 15½×10½×1-inch jelly-roll pan.

2. Stir together brown sugar, butter and granulated sugar in large bowl; beat in eggs and vanilla. Add flour and salt, beating just until blended. Stir in 1½ cups chips; spread batter in prepared pan.

3. Bake 25 to 30 minutes or until wooden pick inserted in center comes out clean and surface is lightly browned. Cool completely; cut into bars.

4. Place remaining ¼ cup chips and shortening in small microwave-safe bowl. Microwave at HIGH (100%) 30 seconds; stir. If necessary, microwave at HIGH an additional 15 seconds at a time, stirring after each heating, until chips are melted and mixture is smooth when stirred. Drizzle over bars.

Makes about 6 dozen bars

Toffee-Top Cheesecake Bars

Almond-Orange Shortbread

1 cup (4 ounces) sliced almonds, divided
2 cups all-purpose flour
1 cup (2 sticks) cold butter, cut into pieces
½ cup sugar
½ cup cornstarch
2 tablespoons grated orange peel
1 teaspoon almond extract

1. Preheat oven to 350°F. Spread ¾ cup almonds in single layer in large baking pan. Bake 6 minutes or until golden brown, stirring frequently. Cool completely in pan. *Reduce oven temperature to 325°F.*

2. Place toasted almonds in food processor. Process using on/off pulses until almonds are coarsely chopped.

3. Add flour, butter, sugar, cornstarch, orange peel and almond extract to food processor. Process using on/off pulses until mixture resembles coarse crumbs.

4. Press dough firmly and evenly into 10×8¾-inch rectangle on large ungreased cookie sheet. Score dough into 1¼-inch squares. Press one slice of remaining almonds in center of each square.

5. Bake 30 to 40 minutes or until shortbread is firm when pressed and lightly browned.

6. Immediately cut into squares along score lines with sharp knife. Remove cookies to wire racks; cool completely.

7. Store loosely covered at room temperature up to 1 week. *Makes about 4½ dozen cookies*

Green's Butterscotch Blondies

½ cup (1 stick) butter, softened
¾ cup granulated sugar
¾ cup firmly packed light brown sugar
2 eggs
1½ teaspoons vanilla extract
1½ cups all-purpose flour
1 teaspoon baking powder
½ teaspoon salt
1¼ cups "M&M's"® Semi-Sweet Chocolate Mini Baking Bits, divided
½ cup butterscotch chips
½ cup chopped pecans
¼ cup caramel ice cream topping

Preheat oven to 350°F. Lightly grease 13×9-inch baking pan; set aside. In large bowl beat butter and sugars until light and fluffy; beat in eggs and vanilla. In medium bowl combine flour, baking powder and salt; add to creamed mixture. Stir in 1 cup "M&M's"® Semi-Sweet Chocolate Mini Baking Bits, butterscotch chips and pecans. Spread in prepared pan. Drop spoonfuls of caramel topping on batter; swirl with knife to marble. Sprinkle with remaining ¼ cup "M&M's"® Semi-Sweet Chocolate Mini Baking Bits. Bake about 25 minutes or until golden brown. Remove pan to wire rack; cool completely. Cut into bars. Store in tightly covered container. *Makes 3 dozen blondies*

Almond-Orange Shortbread

Reese's® Peanut Butter and Milk Chocolate Chip Brownies

¾ **cup HERSHEY'S® Cocoa**
½ **teaspoon baking soda**
⅔ **cup butter or margarine, melted and divided**
½ **cup boiling water**
2 **cups sugar**
2 **eggs**
1⅓ **cups all-purpose flour**
1 **teaspoon vanilla extract**
¼ **teaspoon salt**
1¾ **cups (11-ounce package) REESE'S® Peanut Butter and Milk Chocolate Chips**

1. Heat oven to 350°F. Grease 13×9×2-inch baking pan.

2. Stir together cocoa and baking soda in large bowl; stir in ⅓ cup melted butter. Add boiling water; stir until mixture thickens. Stir in sugar, eggs and remaining ⅓ cup melted butter; stir until smooth. Add flour, vanilla and salt; blend thoroughly. Stir in chips. Pour into prepared pan.

3. Bake 35 to 40 minutes or until brownies begin to pull away from sides of pan. Cool completely in pan on wire rack. Cut into squares.
Makes about 36 brownies

Rocky Road Brownies

½ **cup (1 stick) butter**
½ **cup unsweetened cocoa powder**
1 **cup sugar**
½ **cup all-purpose flour**
¼ **cup buttermilk**
1 **egg**
1 **teaspoon vanilla**
1 **cup miniature marshmallows**
1 **cup coarsely chopped walnuts**
1 **cup (6 ounces) semisweet chocolate chips**

1. Preheat oven to 350°F. Lightly grease 8-inch square pan.

2. Combine butter and cocoa in medium saucepan over low heat, stirring constantly until smooth. Remove from heat; stir in sugar, flour, buttermilk, egg and vanilla. Mix until smooth. Spread batter evenly in prepared pan.

3. Bake 25 minutes or until center feels dry. *Do not overbake or brownies will be dry.* Remove from oven; sprinkle with marshmallows, walnuts and chocolate chips. Return to oven 3 to 5 minutes or just until topping is slightly melted. Cool in pan on wire rack. Cut into 2-inch squares.
Makes 16 brownies

Reese's® Peanut Butter and Milk Chocolate Chip Brownies

Chocolate Orange Gems

⅔ cup butter-flavored solid vegetable
   shortening
¾ cup firmly packed light brown sugar
1 egg
¼ cup orange juice
1 tablespoon grated orange zest
2¼ cups all-purpose flour
½ teaspoon baking powder
½ teaspoon baking soda
½ teaspoon salt
1¾ cups "M&M's"® Chocolate Mini Baking
   Bits
1 cup coarsely chopped pecans
⅓ cup orange marmalade
   Vanilla Glaze (recipe follows)

Preheat oven to 350°F. In large bowl cream shortening and sugar until light and fluffy; beat in egg, orange juice and orange zest. In medium bowl combine flour, baking powder, baking soda and salt; blend into creamed mixture. Stir in "M&M's"® Chocolate Mini Baking Bits and nuts. Reserve 1 cup dough; spread remaining dough in ungreased 13×9×2-inch baking pan. Spread marmalade evenly over top of dough to within ½ inch of edges. Drop reserved dough by teaspoonfuls randomly over marmalade. Bake 25 to 30 minutes or until light golden brown. *Do not overbake.* Cool completely; drizzle with Vanilla Glaze. Cut into bars. Store in tightly covered container.   *Makes 24 bars*

Vanilla Glaze: Combine 1 cup powdered sugar and 1 to 1½ tablespoons warm water until desired consistency. Place glaze in resealable plastic sandwich bag; seal bag. Cut a tiny piece off one corner of the bag (not more than ⅛ inch). Drizzle glaze over cookies.

Fabulous Blonde Brownies

1¾ cups all-purpose flour
1 teaspoon baking powder
¼ teaspoon salt
1 cup (6 ounces) white chocolate chips
1 cup (4 ounces) blanched whole almonds,
   coarsely chopped
1 cup toffee baking pieces
1½ cups packed light brown sugar
⅔ cup butter, softened
2 eggs
2 teaspoons vanilla

1. Preheat oven to 350°F. Lightly grease 13×9-inch baking pan.

2. Combine flour, baking powder and salt in small bowl; mix well. Combine white chocolate chips, almonds and toffee pieces in medium bowl; mix well.

3. Beat brown sugar and butter in large bowl with electric mixer at medium speed until light and fluffy. Beat in eggs and vanilla. Add flour mixture; beat at low speed until well blended. Stir in ¾ cup of white chocolate chip mixture. Spread evenly in prepared pan.

4. Bake 20 minutes. Immediately sprinkle remaining white chocolate chip mixture evenly over brownies. Press down lightly. Bake 15 to 20 minutes or until toothpick inserted into center comes out clean. Cool brownies completely in pan on wire rack. Cut into 2×1½-inch bars.
Makes 3 dozen brownies

Chocolate Orange Gems

Peanut Butter Chip Triangles

1½ cups all-purpose flour
½ cup packed light brown sugar
½ cup (1 stick) cold butter or margarine
1⅔ cups (10-ounce package) REESE'S®
    Peanut Butter Chips, divided
1 can (14 ounces) sweetened condensed
    milk (not evaporated milk)
1 egg, lightly beaten
1 teaspoon vanilla extract
¾ cup chopped walnuts
    Powdered sugar (optional)

1. Heat oven to 350°F. Stir together flour and brown sugar in medium bowl. Cut in butter with pastry blender or fork until mixture resembles coarse crumbs. Stir in ½ cup peanut butter chips. Press mixture onto bottom of ungreased 13×9×2-inch baking pan. Bake 15 minutes.

2. Meanwhile, combine sweetened condensed milk, egg and vanilla in large bowl. Stir in remaining chips and walnuts. Spread evenly over hot baked crust.

3. Bake 25 minutes or until golden brown. Cool completely in pan on wire rack. Cut into 2- or 2½-inch squares; cut squares diagonally into triangles. Sift powdered sugar over top, if desired. *Makes 24 or 40 triangles*

Tip: To sprinkle powdered sugar over brownies, bars, cupcakes or other desserts, place sugar in a wire mesh strainer. Hold over top of desserts and gently tap sides of strainer.

Black Russian Brownies

4 squares (1 ounce each) unsweetened
    chocolate
1 cup butter
¾ teaspoon ground black pepper
4 eggs, lightly beaten
1½ cups granulated sugar
1½ teaspoons vanilla
⅓ cup KAHLÚA® Liqueur
2 tablespoons vodka
1⅓ cups all-purpose flour
½ teaspoon salt
¼ teaspoon baking powder
1 cup chopped walnuts or toasted sliced
    almonds
    Powdered sugar (optional)

Preheat oven to 350°F. Line bottom of 13×9-inch baking pan with waxed paper. Melt chocolate and butter with pepper in small saucepan over low heat, stirring until smooth. Remove from heat; cool.

Combine eggs, granulated sugar and vanilla in large bowl; beat well. Stir in cooled chocolate mixture, Kahlúa and vodka. Combine flour, salt and baking powder; add to chocolate mixture and stir until blended. Add walnuts. Spread evenly in prepared pan.

Bake just until wooden toothpick inserted into center comes out clean, about 25 minutes. *Do not overbake.* Cool in pan on wire rack. Cut into bars. Sprinkle with powdered sugar.
Makes about 2½ dozen brownies

Peanut Butter Chip Triangles

Marvelous Muffins & Breads

Make someone's morning

with a basket of fresh-baked

muffins or a delicious loaf

of quick bread. Package

these treats with a tasty

jam, flavored butter or

gourmet coffee and you'll

have a gift that will

brighten their whole day!

158

Rich Cranberry Scones

    3 cups all-purpose flour
    ⅓ cup plus 1 tablespoon sugar, divided
    1 tablespoon baking powder
    ½ teaspoon salt
    ½ cup I CAN'T BELIEVE IT'S NOT BUTTER!®
        Spread
    ¾ cup dried cranberries
    1 cup plus 1 tablespoon whipping or heavy
        cream, divided
    2 eggs

Preheat oven to 450°F.

In large bowl, combine flour, ⅓ cup sugar, baking powder and salt. With pastry blender or 2 knives, cut in I Can't Believe It's Not Butter!® Spread until mixture is size of fine crumbs. Stir in cranberries.

In small bowl, with wire whisk, blend 1 cup cream and eggs. Stir into flour mixture until dough forms. On floured surface, with floured hands, divide dough in half. Press each half into 6-inch circle. Cut each circle into 6 wedges; place on baking sheet. Brush with remaining 1 tablespoon cream, then sprinkle with remaining 1 tablespoon sugar.

Bake 12 minutes or until golden. Serve warm or cool completely on wire rack.

Makes 12 scones

Rich Cranberry Scones

Gingerbread Streusel Raisin Muffins

        1 cup raisins
        ½ cup boiling water
        ⅓ cup margarine or butter, softened
        ¾ cup GRANDMA'S® Molasses
            (Unsulphured)
        1 egg
        2 cups all-purpose flour
     1½ teaspoons baking soda
        1 teaspoon cinnamon
        1 teaspoon ginger
        ½ teaspoon salt
Topping
        ⅓ cup all-purpose flour
        ¼ cup firmly packed brown sugar
        ¼ cup chopped nuts
        3 tablespoons margarine or butter
        1 teaspoon cinnamon

Preheat oven to 375°F. Grease bottoms only of 12 muffin cups or line with paper baking cups. In small bowl, cover raisins with boiling water; let stand 5 minutes. In large bowl, beat ⅓ cup margarine and molasses until fluffy. Add egg; beat well. Stir in 2 cups flour, baking soda, 1 teaspoon cinnamon, ginger and salt. Blend just until dry ingredients are moistened. Gently stir in raisins and water. Fill prepared muffin cups ¾ full. For topping, combine all ingredients in small bowl. Sprinkle over muffins.

Bake 20 to 25 minutes or until toothpick inserted in centers comes out clean. Cool 5 minutes; remove from pan. Serve warm.

Makes 12 muffins

Banana Walnut Bread

        ⅔ cup sugar
        ⅓ cup butter or margarine
        ¾ teaspoon grated lemon peel
        1 egg
     1¼ cups flour
        ¾ cup ground California walnuts
     1½ teaspoons baking powder
        ¼ teaspoon baking soda
     1⅓ cups mashed ripe bananas (about 3)
        ½ cup chopped California walnuts

In mixing bowl, cream sugar, butter and lemon peel. Beat in egg. Combine flour, ground walnuts, baking powder and baking soda. Add to creamed mixture alternately with bananas, blending thoroughly after each addition. Stir in chopped walnuts. Pour batter into greased 8½×4½-inch loaf pan. Bake in preheated 350°F oven 50 to 55 minutes or until golden brown and toothpick inserted in center comes out clean. Remove from pan. Cool on rack before slicing.

Makes 1 loaf (10 slices)

Favorite recipe from **Walnut Marketing Board**

Gingerbread Streusel Raisin Muffins

Basic Cream Scones

2¼ cups all-purpose flour
¼ cup granulated sugar
1 tablespoon baking powder
½ teaspoon salt
6 tablespoons cold unsalted butter, cut
　　into 6 pieces
⅔ cup heavy cream
2 eggs, beaten
Coarse decorating sugar

1. Preheat oven to 425°F. Fit food processor with steel blade. Place flour, sugar, baking powder and salt in work bowl. Pulse on/off to mix. Add butter; process 10 seconds or until mixture resembles coarse crumbs. Transfer to large bowl.

2. Mix cream and eggs. Reserve 1 tablespoon mixture. Pour remaining cream mixture over flour mixture. Stir just until dry ingredients are moistened and dough is soft.

3. Turn out dough onto lightly floured surface. Shape into ball; pat into 8-inch circle. Cut into 8 wedges; place 2 inches apart on ungreased baking sheet. Brush reserved cream mixture over tops; sprinkle with coarse sugar.

4. Bake 12 to 14 minutes or until golden. Transfer to wire rack to cool.　　*Makes 8 servings*

Chocolate Lavender Scones: Add 1 teaspoon dried lavender to dry ingredients. Coarsely chop 3 (1-ounce) squares semisweet baking chocolate (about ½ cup); stir into dough before shaping.

Ginger Peach Scones: Stir 1 tablespoon finely chopped crystallized ginger and ⅓ cup chopped dried peaches into dough before shaping.

Lemon Poppyseed Scones: Stir grated rind of 1 lemon (about 3½ teaspoons) and 1 tablespoon poppy seeds into dough before shaping. Omit coarse sugar topping. When scones have cooled slightly, drizzle with lemon icing made from 1 cup powdered sugar and 2 tablespoons lemon juice (add up to 1½ teaspoons more lemon juice, if necessary, for desired consistency).

Maple Pecan Scones: Stir ½ cup coarsely chopped pecans into dough before shaping. Omit coarse sugar topping. When scones have cooled slightly, drizzle with maple icing made from ¾ cup powdered sugar and 2 tablespoons maple syrup.

Helpful Hint

Unsalted butter has a more delicate flavor than salted butter and is preferred by many cooks, especially for sauces and baking. Although it varies by manufacturer, salted butter has about 1½ teaspoons of added salt per pound.

From left: Ginger Peach Scones, Lemon Poppyseed Scones, Chocolate Lavender Scones and Maple Pecan Scones

Fudgey Peanut Butter Chip Muffins

½ **cup applesauce**
½ **cup quick-cooking rolled oats**
¼ **cup (½ stick) butter or margarine,
      softened**
½ **cup granulated sugar**
½ **cup packed light brown sugar**
 1 **egg**
½ **teaspoon vanilla extract**
¾ **cup all-purpose flour**
¼ **cup HERSHEY'S Dutch Processed Cocoa
      or HERSHEY'S Cocoa**
½ **teaspoon baking soda**
¼ **teaspoon ground cinnamon (optional)**
 1 **cup REESE'S® Peanut Butter Chips
      Powdered sugar (optional)**

1. Heat oven to 350°F. Line muffin cups
(2½ inches in diameter) with paper baking cups.

2. Stir together applesauce and oats in small
bowl; set aside. Beat butter, granulated sugar,
brown sugar, egg and vanilla in large bowl until
well blended. Add applesauce mixture; blend
well. Stir together flour, cocoa, baking soda and
cinnamon, if desired. Add to butter mixture,
blending well. Stir in peanut butter chips. Fill
muffin cups ¾ full with batter.

3. Bake 22 to 26 minutes or until wooden pick
inserted in center comes out almost clean. Cool
slightly in pan on wire rack. Sprinkle muffin tops
with powdered sugar, if desired. Serve warm.
Makes 12 to 15 muffins

Fudgey Chocolate Chip Muffins: Omit
Peanut Butter Chips. Add 1 cup HERSHEY'S
Semi-Sweet Chocolate Chips.

Cherries and Cream Muffins

2½ **cups frozen unsweetened tart cherries,
      divided**
 1 **cup granulated sugar**
½ **cup butter or margarine**
 2 **eggs**
 1 **teaspoon almond extract**
½ **teaspoon vanilla extract**
 2 **cups all-purpose flour**
 2 **teaspoons baking powder**
½ **teaspoon salt**
½ **cup light cream, half-and-half or milk**

Cut cherries into halves while frozen. Set aside
to thaw and drain. In large bowl, beat sugar and
butter until light and fluffy. Add eggs, almond
extract and vanilla, beating well. Crush ½ cup
cherries with fork; stir into batter.

Combine flour, baking powder and salt. Fold
half the flour mixture into batter with spatula,
then half the cream. Fold in remaining flour and
cream. Fold in remaining cherry halves. Portion
batter evenly into 12 paper-lined or lightly
greased muffin cups (2¾ inches in diameter).
Sprinkle with additional sugar.

Bake in preheated 375°F oven 20 to 30 minutes
or until golden brown.   *Makes 12 muffins*

Favorite recipe from **Cherry Marketing Institute**

Fudgey Peanut Butter Chip Muffins

Sun-Dried Tomato Scones

> 2 cups buttermilk baking mix
> ¼ cup (1 ounce) grated Parmesan cheese
> 1½ teaspoons dried basil leaves
> ⅔ cup reduced-fat (2%) milk
> ½ cup chopped drained oil-packed
>   sun-dried tomatoes
> ¼ cup chopped green onions

1. Preheat oven to 450°F. Combine baking mix, cheese and basil in medium bowl.

2. Stir in milk, tomatoes and onions. Mix just until dry ingredients are moistened. Drop by heaping teaspoonfuls onto greased baking sheet.

3. Bake 8 to 10 minutes or until light golden brown. Remove baking sheet to cooling rack; let stand 5 minutes. Remove scones and serve warm or at room temperature.

Makes 1½ dozen scones

Sun-Dried Tomato Scones

Mini Pumpkin Cranberry Breads

> 3 cups all-purpose flour
> 1 tablespoon plus 2 teaspoons pumpkin
>   pie spice
> 2 teaspoons baking soda
> 1½ teaspoons salt
> 3 cups granulated sugar
> 1 can (15 ounces) LIBBY'S® 100% Pure
>   Pumpkin
> 4 eggs
> 1 cup vegetable oil
> ½ cup orange juice or water
> 1 cup sweetened dried, fresh or frozen
>   cranberries

PREHEAT oven to 350°F. Grease and flour five or six 5×3-inch mini disposable or meat loaf pans.

COMBINE flour, pumpkin pie spice, baking soda and salt in large bowl. Combine sugar, pumpkin, eggs, vegetable oil and orange juice in large mixer bowl; beat until just blended. Add pumpkin mixture to flour mixture; stir just until moistened. Fold in cranberries. Spoon batter into prepared loaf pans.

BAKE for 50 to 55 minutes or until wooden pick inserted in center comes out clean. Cool in pans on wire racks for 10 minutes; remove to wire racks to cool completely.

Makes 5 or 6 mini loaves

Mini Pumpkin Cranberry Bread

Cheddar Olive Scones

2 cups all-purpose flour
1½ cups (6 ounces) shredded sharp Cheddar cheese
1 tablespoon sugar
2 teaspoons baking powder
1½ teaspoons cumin seed
¾ cup sour cream
¼ cup salad oil
1 egg
½ cup pitted California ripe olives, cut into wedges

Mix flour, cheese, sugar, baking powder and cumin in large bowl. Beat sour cream, oil and egg in small bowl. Add egg mixture to flour mixture; stir just enough to moisten evenly. Gently stir in olives. Scrape dough onto lightly greased 15×10-inch baking sheet. Lightly flour hands; pat dough into 1-inch-thick round with lightly floured fingers. Cut round into 8 wedges with knife. Bake in preheated 375°F oven 30 to 35 minutes or until well browned. Serve warm or at room temperature. Cut or break scones into wedges. *Makes 8 servings*

Favorite recipe from **California Olive Industry**

Anjou Pear Cheese Muffins

2 cups all-purpose flour
¼ cup packed brown sugar
3 teaspoons baking powder
½ teaspoon salt
¾ cup (3 ounces) shredded Swiss cheese
⅔ cup milk
1 egg, lightly beaten
2 tablespoons vegetable oil
1 USA Anjou pear, cored and finely chopped
½ cup chopped nuts

Preheat oven to 400°F. Grease 12 (2½-inch) muffin cups; set aside.

Combine flour, sugar, baking powder, salt and cheese in large bowl. Combine milk, egg and oil in small bowl. Stir into flour mixture with pear and nuts just until moistened. Spoon evenly into prepared muffin cups.

Bake 20 to 25 minutes or until wooden pick inserted in center comes out clean. Cool on wire rack 10 minutes. Serve warm or cool completely. *Makes 12 muffins*

Note: Anjou Pear Cheese Muffins can be frozen in aluminum foil or plastic food storage bags. Reheat, unthawed, at 350°F 20 to 25 minutes or until thoroughly heated.

Favorite recipe from **Pear Bureau Northwest**

Tex-Mex Quick Bread

1½ cups all-purpose flour
1 cup (4 ounces) shredded Monterey Jack cheese
½ cup cornmeal
½ cup sun-dried tomatoes, coarsely chopped
1 can (about 4 ounces) black olives, drained and chopped
¼ cup sugar
1½ teaspoons baking powder
1 teaspoon baking soda
1 cup milk
1 can (about 4 ounces) green chilies, drained and chopped
¼ cup olive oil
1 egg, beaten

1. Preheat oven to 325°F. Grease 9×5-inch loaf pan or four 5×3-inch loaf pans; set aside.

2. Combine flour, cheese, cornmeal, tomatoes, olives, sugar, baking powder and baking soda in large bowl.

3. Combine remaining ingredients in small bowl. Stir into flour mixture just until dry ingredients are moistened. Pour into prepared pan. Bake 9×5-inch loaf 45 minutes and 5×3-inch loaves 30 minutes or until toothpick inserted near center of loaf comes out clean. Cool in pan 15 minutes. Remove from pan and cool completely on wire rack.   *Makes 1 large loaf or 4 small loaves*

Muffin Variation: Preheat oven to 375°F. Spoon batter into 12 well-greased muffin pan cups. Bake 20 minutes or until toothpicks inserted into centers come out clean. Makes 12 muffins.

Raspberry Breakfast Braid

Braid
2 cups packaged baking mix
1 (3-ounce) package cream cheese
¼ cup butter or margarine
⅓ cup milk
½ cup SMUCKER'S® Red Raspberry Preserves
Glaze
1 cup powdered sugar
¼ teaspoon almond extract
¼ teaspoon vanilla
1 to 2 tablespoons milk

1. Place baking mix in medium bowl. Cut in cream cheese and butter until mixture is crumbly. Stir in milk. Turn dough onto lightly floured surface and knead lightly 10 to 12 times. Roll dough into 12×8-inch rectangle. Transfer to greased baking sheet. Spread preserves lengthwise down center ⅓ of dough. Make 2½-inch cuts at 1-inch intervals on long sides. Fold strips over filling.

2. Bake at 425°F for 12 to 15 minutes or until lightly browned.

3. Combine all glaze ingredients, adding enough milk for desired drizzling consistency. Drizzle over coffeecake.   *Makes 10 to 12 servings*

Donna's Heavenly Orange Chip Scones

- **4 cups all-purpose flour**
- **1 cup granulated sugar**
- **4 teaspoons baking powder**
- **½ teaspoon baking soda**
- **½ teaspoon salt**
- **1 cup (6 ounces) NESTLÉ® TOLL HOUSE® Semi-Sweet Chocolate Mini Morsels**
- **1 cup golden raisins**
- **1 tablespoon grated orange peel**
- **1 cup (2 sticks) unsalted butter, cut into pieces and softened**
- **1 cup buttermilk**
- **3 eggs, *divided***
- **1 teaspoon orange extract**
- **1 tablespoon milk**
  Icing (recipe follows)

PREHEAT oven to 350°F. Lightly grease baking sheets.

COMBINE flour, granulated sugar, baking powder, baking soda and salt in large bowl. Add morsels, raisins and orange peel; mix well. Cut in butter with pastry blender or two knives until mixture resembles coarse crumbs. Combine buttermilk, *2 eggs* and orange extract in small bowl. Pour buttermilk mixture into flour mixture; mix just until a sticky dough is formed. Do not overmix. Drop by ¼ cupfuls onto prepared baking sheets. Combine *remaining* egg and milk in small bowl. Brush egg mixture over top of dough.

BAKE for 18 to 22 minutes or until wooden pick inserted in center comes out clean. For best results, bake one baking sheet at a time. Cool on wire racks for 10 minutes. Drizzle scones with icing. Serve warm.   *Makes 2 dozen scones*

Icing: COMBINE 2 cups powdered sugar, ¼ cup orange juice, 1 tablespoon grated orange peel and 1 teaspoon orange extract in medium bowl. Mix until smooth.

Savory Cheddar Bread

- **2 cups all-purpose flour**
- **4 teaspoons baking powder**
- **1 tablespoon sugar**
- **½ teaspoon onion salt**
- **½ teaspoon oregano, crushed**
- **¼ teaspoon dry mustard**
- **1 cup (4 ounces) SARGENTO® Fancy Mild or Sharp Cheddar Shredded Cheese**
- **1 egg, beaten**
- **1 cup milk**
- **1 tablespoon butter or margarine, melted**

In large bowl, stir together flour, baking powder, sugar, onion salt, oregano, dry mustard and cheese. In separate bowl, combine egg, milk and melted butter; add to dry ingredients, stirring just until moistened. Spread batter in greased 8×4-inch loaf pan. Bake at 350°F 45 minutes or until wooden pick inserted in center comes out clean. Cool 10 minutes on wire rack. Remove from pan.   *Makes 16 slices*

Donna's Heavenly Orange Chip Scones

Aloha Bread

1 (10-ounce) jar maraschino cherries
1¾ cups all-purpose flour
2 teaspoons baking powder
½ teaspoon salt
⅔ cup firmly packed brown sugar
⅓ cup butter or margarine, softened
2 eggs
1 cup mashed ripe bananas
½ cup chopped macadamia nuts or
   walnuts

Drain maraschino cherries, reserving
2 tablespoons juice. Cut cherries into quarters;
set aside.

Combine flour, baking powder and salt in small
bowl; set aside.

In medium bowl, combine brown sugar, butter,
eggs and reserved cherry juice; mix on medium
speed of electric mixer until ingredients are
thoroughly combined. Add flour mixture
alternately with mashed bananas, beginning
and ending with flour mixture. Stir in cherries
and nuts. Lightly spray 9×5×3-inch loaf pan
with nonstick cooking spray. Spread batter
evenly in pan.

Bake in preheated 350°F oven 1 hour or until
loaf is golden brown and wooden pick inserted
near center comes out clean. Remove from pan
and cool on wire rack. Store in tightly covered
container or foil.   *Makes 1 loaf (about 16 slices)*

Favorite recipe from **Cherry Marketing Institute**

Pineapple-Raisin Muffins

¼ cup finely chopped pecans
¼ cup packed light brown sugar
2 cups all-purpose flour
¼ cup granulated sugar
2½ teaspoons baking powder
¾ teaspoon salt
½ teaspoon ground cinnamon
6 tablespoons cold butter
½ cup raisins
1 can (8 ounces) crushed pineapple in
   juice, undrained
⅓ cup unsweetened pineapple juice
1 egg

1. Preheat oven to 400°F. Lightly grease
12 standard (2½-inch) muffin pan cups or line
with paper baking cups.

2. Combine pecans and brown sugar in small
bowl; set aside. Combine flour, granulated sugar,
baking powder, salt and cinnamon in large bowl.
Cut in butter with pastry blender or 2 knives until
mixture resembles fine crumbs. Stir in raisins.

3. Combine crushed pineapple with juice,
pineapple juice and egg in small bowl; stir until
blended. Add to flour mixture; stir just until
moistened. Spoon batter evenly into prepared
muffin cups, filling ⅔ full. Sprinkle with pecan
mixture.

4. Bake 20 to 25 minutes or until golden brown
and toothpicks inserted into centers come out
clean. Immediately remove from pan; cool on
wire rack 10 minutes. Serve warm or at room
temperature.   *Makes 12 muffins*

Aloha Bread

Mocha-Macadamia Nut Muffins

1¼ cups all-purpose flour
⅔ cup granulated sugar
2½ tablespoons unsweetened cocoa powder
1 teaspoon baking soda
¼ teaspoon salt
⅔ cup buttermilk*
3 tablespoons margarine or butter, melted
1 egg, beaten
1 tablespoon instant coffee granules dissolved in 1 tablespoon hot water
¾ teaspoon vanilla
½ cup coarsely chopped macadamia nuts
Powdered sugar (optional)

Soured fresh milk can be substituted for buttermilk. To sour milk, combine 2 teaspoons lemon juice plus enough milk to equal ⅔ cup. Stir; let stand 5 minutes before using.

1. Preheat oven to 400°F. Lightly grease 12 standard (2½-inch) muffin pan cups or line with paper baking cups.

2. Combine flour, granulated sugar, cocoa, baking soda and salt in large bowl. Combine buttermilk, melted margarine, egg, coffee mixture and vanilla in medium bowl; beat until blended. Stir buttermilk mixture into flour mixture just until dry ingredients are moistened. Stir in macadamia nuts. Spoon batter evenly into prepared muffin cups.

3. Bake 13 to 17 minutes or until toothpicks inserted into centers come out clean. Cool in pan on wire rack 5 minutes. Remove from pan to wire rack; cool 10 minutes. Sprinkle with powdered sugar, if desired. *Makes 12 muffins*

Lemon Cranberry Loaves

1¼ cups finely chopped fresh cranberries
½ cup finely chopped walnuts
¼ cup granulated sugar
1 package DUNCAN HINES® Moist Deluxe® Lemon Supreme Cake Mix
¾ cup milk
1 package (3 ounces) cream cheese, softened
4 eggs
Confectioners' sugar

1. Preheat oven to 350°F. Grease and flour two 8½×4½-inch loaf pans.

2. Stir together cranberries, walnuts and granulated sugar in large bowl; set aside.

3. Combine cake mix, milk and cream cheese in large bowl. Beat at medium speed with electric mixer for 2 minutes. Add eggs, 1 at a time, beating for 2 minutes. Fold in cranberry mixture. Pour into prepared pans. Bake at 350°F for 45 to 50 minutes or until toothpick inserted in centers comes out clean. Cool in pans 15 minutes. Loosen loaves from pans. Invert onto cooling rack. Turn right side up. Cool completely. Dust with confectioners' sugar. *Makes 24 slices*

Tip: To quickly chop cranberries or walnuts, use a food processor fitted with a steel blade and pulse until evenly chopped.

Mocha-Macadamia Nut Muffins

Star-Of-The-East Fruit Bread

½ cup (1 stick) butter or margarine,
  softened
1 cup sugar
2 eggs
1 teaspoon vanilla extract
2 cups all-purpose flour
1 teaspoon baking soda
¼ teaspoon salt
1 cup mashed ripe bananas (about
  3 medium)
1 can (11 ounces) mandarin orange
  segments, well-drained
1 cup HERSHEY'S Semi-Sweet Chocolate
  Chips
½ cup chopped dates or Calimyrna figs
½ cup chopped maraschino cherries,
  well-drained
  Chocolate Drizzle (recipe follows)

1. Heat oven to 350°F. Lightly grease two
8½×4½×2⅝-inch loaf pans.

2. Beat butter and sugar in large bowl until
fluffy. Add eggs and vanilla; beat well. Stir
together flour, baking soda and salt; add
alternately with mashed bananas to butter
mixture, blending well. Stir in orange segments,
chocolate chips, dates and cherries. Divide
batter evenly between prepared pans.

3. Bake 40 to 50 minutes or until golden brown.
Cool; remove from pans. Drizzle tops of loaves
with Chocolate Drizzle. Store tightly wrapped.

Makes 2 loaves

Chocolate Drizzle: Combine ½ cup
HERSHEY'S Semi-Sweet Chocolate Chips and
2 tablespoons whipping cream in small
microwave-safe bowl. Microwave at HIGH
(100%) 30 seconds; stir. If necessary,
microwave at HIGH an additional 15 seconds;
stir until chips are melted and mixture is smooth
when stirred. Makes about ½ cup.

Banana Scotch Muffins

1 ripe, large DOLE® Banana, peeled
1 egg, beaten
½ cup sugar
¼ cup milk
¼ cup vegetable oil
1 teaspoon vanilla
1 cup all-purpose flour
1 cup quick-cooking rolled oats
1 teaspoon baking powder
½ teaspoon baking soda
½ teaspoon salt
½ cup butterscotch chips

• Preheat oven to 400°F. Purée banana in
blender (⅔ cup). In medium bowl, combine
puréed banana, egg, sugar, milk, oil and vanilla.

• In large bowl, combine flour, oats, baking
powder, baking soda and salt. Stir banana
mixture and butterscotch chips into dry
ingredients just until blended.

• Spoon into well-greased 2½-inch muffin pan
cups. Bake 12 to 15 minutes. Remove from pan.

Makes 12 muffins

Star-Of-The-East Fruit Bread

Date Nut Bread

   2 cups all-purpose flour
   ½ cup packed light brown sugar
   1 tablespoon baking powder
   ½ teaspoon salt
   ¼ cup cold butter
   1 cup toasted chopped walnuts
   1 cup chopped dates
1¼ cups milk
   1 egg
   ½ teaspoon grated lemon peel

1. Preheat oven to 375°F. Spray 9×5-inch loaf pan with nonstick cooking spray; set aside.

2. Combine flour, brown sugar, baking powder and salt in large bowl. Cut in butter with pastry blender or 2 knives until mixture resembles fine crumbs. Add walnuts and dates; stir until coated. Beat milk, egg and lemon peel in small bowl with fork. Add to flour mixture; stir just until moistened. Spread in prepared pan.

3. Bake 45 to 50 minutes or until toothpick inserted into center comes out clean. Cool in pan on wire rack 10 minutes. Remove from pan and cool completely on wire rack.

Makes 12 servings

Fruit Muffins

Muffins
   ⅔ cup milk
   1 tablespoon CRISCO® Oil
   1 egg
   2 cups packaged baking mix
   2 tablespoons granulated sugar
   ¼ cup SMUCKER'S® Preserves (any flavor)
Glaze
   ⅔ cup powdered sugar
   3 to 4 teaspoons milk

Grease bottom only of 12 medium muffin cups or line with paper baking cups. Combine milk, oil and egg; stir until well mixed. Add baking mix and granulated sugar; stir just until moistened. Fill prepared muffin cups ⅔ full. Drop 1 level teaspoon preserves onto center of batter in each cup.

Bake at 400°F for 13 to 18 minutes or until golden brown. Cool slightly; remove from pan.

Stir together glaze ingredients until smooth, adding enough milk for desired glaze consistency. Drizzle over cooled muffins.

Makes 12 muffins

Pecan Peach Muffins

Topping (recipe follows)
1½ cups all-purpose flour
½ cup granulated sugar
2 teaspoons baking powder
1 teaspoon ground cinnamon
¼ teaspoon salt
½ cup butter, melted
¼ cup milk
1 egg
2 medium peaches, peeled and diced
(about 1 cup)

1. Preheat oven to 400°F. Line 12 standard (2½-inch) muffin pan cups with paper baking cups or lightly grease.* Prepare Topping; set aside.

2. Combine flour, granulated sugar, baking powder, cinnamon and salt in large bowl. Combine melted butter, milk and egg in small bowl until blended; stir into flour mixture just until dry ingredients are moistened. Fold in peaches. Spoon evenly into prepared muffin cups. Sprinkle Topping over tops of muffins.

3. Bake 20 to 25 minutes or until toothpicks inserted into centers come out clean. Remove from pan to wire rack; cool completely.

Makes 12 muffins

*Muffins can be difficult to remove from pan. For best results, use paper baking cups.

Topping: Combine ½ cup chopped pecans, ⅓ cup packed brown sugar, ¼ cup all-purpose flour and 1 teaspoon ground cinnamon in small bowl. Add 2 tablespoons melted butter or margarine; stir until mixture is crumbly.

Double Pineapple Bread

¾ cup sugar
½ cup margarine, softened
2 eggs
2 cans (8 ounces each) DOLE® Crushed
Pineapple, well drained
1 teaspoon vanilla extract
2 cups all-purpose flour
1 teaspoon baking soda
1 teaspoon baking powder
½ teaspoon ground cinnamon
½ teaspoon salt
½ teaspoon ground nutmeg
½ cup chopped walnuts, toasted

• Beat sugar and margarine until light and fluffy. Beat in eggs. Add drained crushed pineapple and vanilla; mix well.

• Combine dry ingredients. Stir in walnuts. Add to pineapple mixture. Stir until moistened.

• Pour batter into 3 mini loaf pans (5½×3 inches) coated with cooking spray. Bake at 350°F 35 to 40 minutes. Cool in pans 15 minutes. Remove from pans; cool completely on wire rack.

Makes 3 mini loaves (10 slices per loaf)

Blueberry White Chip Muffins

    2 cups all-purpose flour
    ½ cup granulated sugar
    ¼ cup packed brown sugar
    2½ teaspoons baking powder
    ½ teaspoon salt
    ¾ cup milk
    1 egg, lightly beaten
    ¼ cup butter or margarine, melted
    ½ teaspoon grated lemon peel
    2 cups (12-ounce package) NESTLÉ® TOLL
        HOUSE® Premier White Morsels,
        divided
    1½ cups fresh or frozen blueberries
        Streusel Topping (recipe follows)

PREHEAT oven to 375°F. Paper-line 18 muffin cups.

COMBINE flour, granulated sugar, brown sugar, baking powder and salt in large bowl. Stir in milk, egg, butter and lemon peel. Stir in *1½ cups* morsels and blueberries. Spoon into prepared muffin cups, filling almost full. Sprinkle with Streusel Topping.

BAKE for 22 to 25 minutes or until wooden pick inserted in center comes out clean. Cool in pans for 5 minutes; remove to wire racks to cool slightly.

PLACE *remaining* morsels in small, *heavy-duty* resealable plastic food storage bag. Microwave on MEDIUM-HIGH (70%) power for 30 seconds; knead. Microwave at additional 10- to 15-second intervals, kneading until smooth. Cut tiny corner from bag; squeeze to drizzle over muffins. Serve warm.   *Makes 18 muffins*

Streusel Topping: COMBINE ⅓ cup granulated sugar, ¼ cup all-purpose flour and ¼ teaspoon ground cinnamon in small bowl. Cut in 3 tablespoons butter or margarine with pastry blender or two knives until mixture resembles coarse crumbs.

Peanut Butter Scones

    2 cups self-rising flour
    ½ cup creamy peanut butter
    2 eggs *or* ½ cup egg substitute
    ¼ cup granulated sugar
    2½ tablespoons oil
    1 teaspoon vanilla
        Cinnamon
        Additional granulated sugar

Preheat oven to 425°F. Mix all the ingredients except cinnamon and additional sugar together using a fork. Turn the dough out onto an ungreased pizza pan. The dough will look lumpy. Using your hands, shape the dough into a 10-inch circle. Cut the circle into 12 wedges and separate each piece so they are about ¼ inch apart. Sprinkle each piece with a mixture of cinnamon and sugar. Bake 10 minutes. Serve plain or with butter and jam.   *Makes 12 scones*

Favorite recipe from **Peanut Advisory Board**

Blueberry White Chip Muffins

Lots o' Chocolate Bread

- **2 cups miniature semisweet chocolate chips, divided**
- **⅔ cup packed light brown sugar**
- **½ cup (1 stick) butter, softened**
- **2 eggs**
- **2½ cups all-purpose flour**
- **1½ cups applesauce**
- **1½ teaspoons vanilla**
- **1 teaspoon baking soda**
- **1 teaspoon baking powder**
- **½ teaspoon salt**
- **1 tablespoon shortening (do not use butter, margarine, spread or oil)**

1. Preheat oven to 350°F. Grease 5 (5½×3-inch) mini loaf pans. Place 1 cup miniature chocolate chips in small microwavable bowl. Microwave at HIGH 1 minute; stir. Microwave for 30-second intervals, stirring after each interval, until chocolate is melted and smooth; set aside.

2. Beat brown sugar and butter in large bowl until creamy. Add melted chocolate and eggs; beat until well blended. Add flour, applesauce, vanilla, baking soda, baking powder and salt; beat until well blended. Stir in ½ cup chocolate chips. Spoon batter into prepared pans.

3. Bake 35 to 40 minutes or until centers crack and are dry to touch. Cool in pans on wire racks 10 minutes. Transfer to racks; cool completely.

4. Place remaining ½ cup chips and shortening in microwavable bowl. Microwave at HIGH 1 minute; stir. Microwave for 30-second intervals, stirring after each interval, until chocolate is melted and mixture is smooth. Drizzle glaze over loaves; let stand until set. *Makes 5 mini loaves*

Cinnamon Scones

- **3 cups all-purpose flour**
- **⅓ cup plus 1 tablespoon sugar**
- **1 tablespoon baking powder**
- **½ teaspoon plus ⅛ teaspoon ground cinnamon, divided**
- **½ teaspoon salt**
- **½ cup (1 stick) I CAN'T BELIEVE IT'S NOT BUTTER!® Spread**
- **¾ cup currants or raisins**
- **1 cup plus 1 tablespoon whipping or heavy cream, divided**
- **2 eggs**

Preheat oven to 450°F.

In large bowl, combine flour, ⅓ cup sugar, baking powder, ½ teaspoon cinnamon and salt. With pastry blender or two knives, cut in I Can't Believe It's Not Butter!® Spread until mixture is size of fine crumbs. Stir in currants.

In small bowl, with wire whisk, beat 1 cup cream and eggs. Stir into flour mixture until dough forms. On floured surface, with floured hands, divide dough in half. Press each half into 6-inch circle. Cut each circle into 6 wedges; place on baking sheet. Brush with remaining 1 tablespoon cream, then sprinkle with remaining 1 tablespoon sugar mixed with remaining ⅛ teaspoon cinnamon.

Bake 12 minutes or until golden. Serve warm with additional I Can't Believe It's Not Butter! Spread or cool completely on wire rack.

Makes 12 scones

Lots o' Chocolate Bread

Golden Apple Buttermilk Bread

1½ cups unsifted all-purpose flour
1 cup whole wheat flour
½ cup natural bran cereal
1 teaspoon baking soda
½ teaspoon baking powder
¼ teaspoon ground ginger
1⅓ cups buttermilk
¾ cup sugar
¼ cup vegetable oil
1 egg
1 teaspoon grated orange peel
1 cup chopped Washington Golden
　　Delicious apples

1. Heat oven to 350°F. Grease 9×5-inch loaf pan. In medium bowl, combine flours, cereal, baking soda, baking powder and ginger. In large bowl, beat together buttermilk, sugar, oil, egg and orange peel.

2. Add flour mixture to buttermilk mixture, stirring just until combined. Fold in apples. Spread batter in prepared pan and bake 45 to 50 minutes or until wooden toothpick inserted into center comes out clean. Cool bread in pan 10 minutes. Remove from pan and cool on wire rack. *Makes 1 loaf (8 servings)*

Favorite recipe from **Washington Apple Commission**

Peanut Butter Bread

2 cups all-purpose flour
½ cup sugar
2 teaspoons baking powder
½ teaspoon baking soda
½ teaspoon salt
1 cup creamy or chunk peanut butter
½ cup KARO® Light or Dark Corn Syrup
2 eggs
1 cup milk

1. Preheat oven to 350°F. Grease and flour 9×5×3-inch loaf pan. In medium bowl, combine flour, sugar, baking powder, baking soda and salt.

2. In large bowl, with mixer at medium speed, beat peanut butter and corn syrup until smooth. Beat in eggs, 1 at a time. Gradually beat in milk. Stir in flour mixture just until moistened. Pour into prepared pan.

3. Bake 50 to 55 minutes or until wooden toothpick inserted in center comes out clean. Cool in pan 10 minutes. Remove from pan; cool on wire rack. *Makes 1 loaf*

Golden Apple Buttermilk Bread

Acknowledgments

The publisher would like to thank the companies and organizations listed below for the use of their recipes and photographs in this publication.

ACH FOOD COMPANIES, INC.
Arm & Hammer Division, Church & Dwight Co., Inc.
California Olive Industry
Cherry Marketing Institute
Crisco is a registered trademark of The J.M. Smucker Company
Dole Food Company, Inc.
Domino® Foods, Inc.
Duncan Hines® and Moist Deluxe® are registered trademarks of Pinnacle Foods Corp.
Eagle Brand® Sweetened Condensed Milk
Fleischmann's® Margarines and Spreads
Grandma's® is a registered trademark of Mott's, LLP
Hershey Foods Corporation
The Hidden Valley® Food Products Company
JOLLY TIME® Pop Corn
Kahlúa® Liqueur
Lawry's® Foods
© Mars, Incorporated 2005
McIlhenny Company (TABASCO® brand Pepper Sauce)
National Honey Board
Nestlé USA
Peanut Advisory Board
Pear Bureau Northwest
Reckitt Benckiser Inc.
Sargento® Foods Inc.
Smucker's® trademark of The J.M. Smucker Company
Sokol and Company
Southeast United Dairy Industry Association, Inc.
The Sugar Association, Inc.
Unilever Foods North America
Walnut Marketing Board
Washington Apple Commission

METRIC CONVERSION CHART

VOLUME MEASUREMENTS (dry)

1/8 teaspoon = 0.5 mL
1/4 teaspoon = 1 mL
1/2 teaspoon = 2 mL
3/4 teaspoon = 4 mL
1 teaspoon = 5 mL
1 tablespoon = 15 mL
2 tablespoons = 30 mL
1/4 cup = 60 mL
1/3 cup = 75 mL
1/2 cup = 125 mL
2/3 cup = 150 mL
3/4 cup = 175 mL
1 cup = 250 mL
2 cups = 1 pint = 500 mL
3 cups = 750 mL
4 cups = 1 quart = 1 L

VOLUME MEASUREMENTS (fluid)

1 fluid ounce (2 tablespoons) = 30 mL
4 fluid ounces (1/2 cup) = 125 mL
8 fluid ounces (1 cup) = 250 mL
12 fluid ounces (1 1/2 cups) = 375 mL
16 fluid ounces (2 cups) = 500 mL

WEIGHTS (mass)

1/2 ounce = 15 g
1 ounce = 30 g
3 ounces = 90 g
4 ounces = 120 g
8 ounces = 225 g
10 ounces = 285 g
12 ounces = 360 g
16 ounces = 1 pound = 450 g

DIMENSIONS

1/16 inch = 2 mm
1/8 inch = 3 mm
1/4 inch = 6 mm
1/2 inch = 1.5 cm
3/4 inch = 2 cm
1 inch = 2.5 cm

OVEN TEMPERATURES

250°F = 120°C
275°F = 140°C
300°F = 150°C
325°F = 160°C
350°F = 180°C
375°F = 190°C
400°F = 200°C
425°F = 220°C
450°F = 230°C

BAKING PAN SIZES

Utensil	Size in Inches/Quarts	Metric Volume	Size in Centimeters
Baking or Cake Pan (square or rectangular)	8×8×2	2 L	20×20×5
	9×9×2	2.5 L	23×23×5
	12×8×2	3 L	30×20×5
	13×9×2	3.5 L	33×23×5
Loaf Pan	8×4×3	1.5 L	20×10×7
	9×5×3	2 L	23×13×7
Round Layer Cake Pan	8×1½	1.2 L	20×4
	9×1½	1.5 L	23×4
Pie Plate	8×1¼	750 mL	20×3
	9×1¼	1 L	23×3
Baking Dish or Casserole	1 quart	1 L	—
	1½ quart	1.5 L	—
	2 quart	2 L	—